Gil Dodds

You are holding a reproduction of an original work that is in the public domain in the United States of America, and possibly other countries. You may freely copy and distribute this work as no entity (individual or corporate) has a copyright on the body of the work. This book may contain prior copyright references, and library stamps (as most of these works were scanned from library copies). These have been scanned and retained as part of the historical artifact.

This book may have occasional imperfections such as missing or blurred pages, poor pictures, errant marks, etc. that were either part of the original artifact, or were introduced by the scanning process. We believe this work is culturally important, and despite the imperfections, have elected to bring it back into print as part of our continuing commitment to the preservation of printed works worldwide. We appreciate your understanding of the imperfections in the preservation process, and hope you enjoy this valuable book.

GIL DODDS
The Flying Parson

by
MEL LARSON

The Evangelical Beacon
4211 N. Hermitage Ave.
Chicago 13, Illinois

This book is manufactured under wartime conditions and in conformity with Government regulations for conserving paper and other materials.

Copyright, 1945, by
The Evangelical Beacon
Chicago

Printed in the United States of America.

Tributes

"Gil Dodds is a fine combination of a great athlete and a great sportsman. He also happens to be one of the greatest competitors we have had in a long time."
GRANTLAND RICE,
Dean of American Sportswriters.

* * *

"To my good friend Gil Dodds for much track and good running and good companionship. . . . May God give you happiness and fame in your chosen profession, the ministry. Your friend for life."
GUNDER HAGG,
Great Swedish track star.

* * *

"I don't know of a finer sportsman than Gil Dodds. His willingness to tour America with Gunder Hagg was a splendid gesture. . . . He is a splendid athlete, sportsman and Christian, and it was a pleasure for me to present him with the Sullivan award for 1943."
L. DI BENEDETTO,
President, Amateur Athletic Union.

* * *

"Stout fella, and a real champion."
JOHN KIERAN,
Former sports editor, The New York Times.

* * *

"Gil Dodds is a great runner and has a great heart. He is one of the best there is along any line."
GREG RICE,
Undefeated world two-mile champion.

* * *

"For bodily exercise profiteth little: but godliness is profitable unto all things . . ." I Tim. 4:8. Gil Dodds has demonstrated on the track his excellence as a champion athlete. He has demonstrated more clearly and effectively in his life and testimony that he is a greater champion for the Lord Jesus Christ. In all of my association with him I have found him to be a man of deepest devotion and consecration to Jesus Christ. His greatness as an athlete will soon be outshone by his even greater accomplishments as a winner of souls.
TORREY M. JOHNSON,
Chairman, National Youth for Christ.

* * *

"Gil Dodds is a modern Spartan, perfectly willing to subject himself to the most exacting regimen."
JACK RYDER,
Track coach, Boston Athletic Association.

* * *

"It has been with considerable personal satisfaction that I have watched the progress of Gil Dodds through his athletic career and to that more important one which he is undertaking. I knew him first as a shy, retiring

boy whose physical endowments were obvious, a boy who needed only opportunity and confidence. If I have helped him in either his chances or his purpose, I feel well rewarded." BILL McKEE,
Sports editor, Ashland Times-Gazette (Ohio).

* * *

"Everyone admires the winner, who by industry and integrity comes to high achievements in human affairs. Here is the story of a winner, the height of whose achievement stands in contrast to his modesty and humility.

"It has been my great pleasure to know Gil Dodds personally, to talk with him on things spiritual and academic, and to find him a Greatheart who loves God and men. He is desperately in earnest about this matter of winning the race from all competitors and also of winning men to Christ. His testimony has thrilled the student body of Wheaton College as it has throngs of young people everywhere in the land. We have seen him run in competition and have rejoiced in his accomplishment. We are glad he is a winner and is a Christian. V. RAYMOND EDMAN, Ph.D., LL.D.,
President, Wheaton College.

* * *

"Known to the sports world as the 'Galloping Parson' and the 'Epistle-packing Pastor,' Gil Dodds has become known to us who love the Saviour as 'Brother Gil,' a dear child of God.

"It was my joy to see Gil many Saturday nights during the 1944 winter season. Early in the evening he would be at our prayer meetings prior to the broadcast. Following our program it was often our privilege to watch him run in Madison Square Garden. We were there the night Gil first broke the world record and we saw that great crowd stand to its feet and applaud him wildly as he finished the race.

"In the summer of 1944 we had the privilege of being with Gil for 55 meetings up and down the East coast. In those meetings and in our every contact it has been a blessing and a challenge to know Gil and to feel his greatness, both as an athlete and a Christian." JACK WYRTZEN,
Director, Word of Life Hour, Times Square, New York.

* * *

"The thing I like about Gil Dodds is — he shows to the world a man can be a good athlete and a good Christian, and he's both!"
PERCY CRAWFORD,
Director, Young Peoples Church of the Air.

* * *

"Gil Dodds is one of the greatest sportsmen I have ever met. He is quiet and unassuming and always does everything possible to assist young athletes. He has devoted a great deal of his time to giving talks on athletics before groups of boys. He is an idol with the youngsters.

"On a four-lap outdoor track under ideal conditions Dodds may run the mile in four minutes. . . . His admirers in all parts of the United States are eager to see him reach this goal." JACK CONWAY,
Sports Editor, Boston American and Boston Sunday Advertiser.

PREFACE

No athlete in modern times has so vividly captured and held the attention and eyes of the American sport fan as Gil Dodds, the unassuming holder of the world indoor mile record of 4:06.4 minutes, winner of the coveted Sullivan Award trophy of 1943, and title-holder in numerous other events. His name has indeed become a household word in the homes of millions of Americans.

As a sports writer on a metropolitan daily, it was my privilege again and again to handle Associated Press, United Press, and International News Service stories from many cities in which Gil Dodds competed. Invariably the competent sports writers paid tribute to the "Scripture-quoting divinity student" from Boston. The way in which those stories were written was proof enough that here was an athlete who had something more than a fine pair of legs.

It was my privilege to watch him under pressure a day before his greatest race in the Chicago Stadium on March 18, 1944, as well as to see him set the world's indoor mile record before 13,286 fans that night. On other occasions we have heard him speak to groups varying in size from a handful to 28,000 at a youth meeting in the same Chicago Stadium where he set his record.

These contacts furnished the inspiration for presenting this story of *Gil Dodds the Christian* and *Gil Dodds the Runner* — the champion who says, "I'd gladly run a mile for Christ."

The Author.

CONTENTS

Chapter

I Two Nights ... Two Meets ... Two Records - 7

II A Stone ... A Lady ... A Decision - - - - 14

III High School ... Hahn ... Honors - - - - 20

IV College ... Crisis .. Cups ... Championships 27

V Boston ... Jack Ryder ... Fame - - - - 40

VI Hagg ... Sullivan Award ... World Record! 50

VII Little Bit of Everything - - - - - - - - 64

VIII Witnessing With His Lips - - - - - - - 87

IX "I Run For Christ!" by Gil Dodds - - - - - 90

Chapter I

TWO NIGHTS ... TWO MEETS ... TWO RECORDS

IT was the usual Saturday night in New York. People were everywhere, and more of them coming. The calendar read "March 11, 1944."

Any place is crowded in New York on a Saturday night and this, being a war year, found it more so.

Not far from Times Square a fellow walked purposefully and yet not hurriedly along. He seemed to be going nowhere, but he wasn't loafing. The clock showed a few minutes after six o'clock. This was "dinner time" to millions of New Yorkers, but this fellow wasn't eating any supper.

Down the street a few blocks, an excited mob already was starting to pour its way into Madison Square Garden, scene that night of the annual Knights of Columbus track meet. Sport fans were keyed for this night. Gil Dodds, the "Flying Parson" from Boston, would be gunning for a new world record in the mile. Four weeks before on this same track he had raced the mile in 4:10.6 minutes. In his next two races he had edged that down to 4:08 minutes flat.

The record was 4:07.4 minutes, held jointly by three men — Glenn Cunningham, Charles Fenske and Leslie MacMitchell. No one in the world had ever run the indoor mile under that figure.

The "man on the street" continued his walking. Soon he came to a building which looked as though it could seat about 1,000 persons. He went inside.

A prayer meeting was in progress. In an hour or so a

—7—

"youth meeting" called the Word of Life Hour, would be going on in this building, conducted by a former jazz band player, Jack Wyrtzen. "The man" joined in the prayer meeting for a short while, then just as quietly slipped out and started back toward his hotel.

The last few hours before an athletic meet are tough on any athlete, and Gil Dodds, though he gets added strength from God in all of his running, is human. The mental and physical strain was noticeable even as he walked along.

He reached his hotel and went up to his room. Other times he had gone to a movie to "rest" his nerves, but one look at Hollywood the summer before had cured him of movies. Tonight he wanted to be alone . . . with God.

No singer, he sang nonetheless. Songs like "Sweet Hour of Prayer," "In the Garden," and "Onward Christian Soldiers" came from his lips. He sat still for a while, then slid down onto his knees for one last prayer meeting.

Then he was on his way to the Garden.

Up in Boston a mother with a month-old baby knelt and prayed that her husband would do his best in New York that night. Spread throughout the land, countless other friends asked God to help Gil Dodds again that night. A few miles from New York, in a naval base, three merchant marine men knelt and prayed, "Lord, let Gil Dodds set a world record tonight."

An hour or so later a world record for the indoor mile was on the record books!

The name that preceded the record was "Gil Dodds, Boston Athletic Association."

The time — 4:07.3 minutes, a new record by one-tenth of a second!

Once more Gilbert Lothair Dodds, 148 pounds of muscle and might, had fulfilled the prediction of Coach Jack Ryder, known the world over as "Maker of Champions." Once more, according to a hard-working press section, the driving, merciless training routine through which Gil Dodds puts himself had paid off in a world record!

But to Gil . . . and to that praying wife in Boston . . . and to many others who had prayed for him . . . that record came because God heard the prayers . . . and answered!

* * *

The scene shifts.

It is a week later and 13,286 fans are packed into Chicago Stadium in the second largest city in the country.

The star-studded meet goes on its way with planned precision. Onto the track comes an obscure-looking athlete in a dark sweat suit.

Gil Dodds has arrived, and as he warms up he nods to friends near the rail in the first row. Once more he looks to be in tip-top shape, but so does Bill Hulse, the man who had pushed him to a record a week before and who has run the mile in 4:06 minutes on the outdoor track.

But let's look back a few hours; almost a day, in fact.

On Friday afternoon Gil Dodds arrived in Chicago from Boston. A long walk loosened up the muscles after the lengthy train ride. At 7 o'clock he ate a heavy, "athletic dinner" after bowing his head with two companions and asking God's blessing on the food about to be eaten. This was one of Chicago's busiest eating places, but there was time to say grace.

After the meal . . . another walk. This one was longer,

but still short enough to put him in bed by 10 p.m., his usual retiring time. Before going to sleep out came a Bible he never leaves out of his reach; a few chapters were read, a lengthy time spent in prayer, and then off to a sound, satisfying sleep.

On Saturday he meets Lloyd Hahn, the man who coached him through high school in person and through college by mail. From distant Falls City, Neb., Hahn had come to be with his former pupil. They talked over old times; they checked Gil's plans for the race as outlined by Jack Ryder before he left Boston.

Things checked all around. Gil was glad to see Lloyd Hahn; he admired and loved his former coach, the man who took him as a green junior in high school and taught him the fundamentals the right way and who himself had won this very same race in which Gil was to compete, the Bankers' Mile, four times when in his prime.

Lloyd Hahn, the mile champ of 1924-1929. He, too, was a Christian—a deacon in his church and a Sunday School teacher.

Back to his hotel room to be alone . . . and to take time to pray. Then to the Stadium . . . and the call for the Banker's Mile!

Up in the balcony at Chicago Stadium that night one of the nation's top vocal soloists, Beverly Shea, and his friends held a prayer meeting that Gil Dodds might run his best that night. Across the country in Boston a young mother prayed the same prayer. In a New York naval base three merchant marine men might have knelt and once more prayed, "Lord, help Gil Dodds tonight to set a record."

The starting gun went off, and if you had watched Gil Dodds closely you would have seen his lips moving in a short, simple, unlearned prayer to God for help in this race.

Seconds ticked off as the laps were covered. Gil was leading, but Bill Hulse wasn't over a step or two behind. On the side of the track Lloyd Hahn knelt and called the lap times to Gil as he rolled steadily along lap after lap.

The Chicago Stadium track measures 11 laps to the mile. At the end of the tenth lap the gun went off, signaling the start of the final lap. Hulse still was only a stride behind. Around the first curve on the final lap they sped.

Suddenly Gil Dodds "let himself out." The distance between himself and Hulse widened . . . and widened. Hulse knew then that barring an accident he couldn't catch Dodds.

The standing crowd was roaring and urging Gil on as he whipped around the final curve and into the stretch drive. His legs were straining and his entire body pounding forward as he finally almost threw himself at the tape . . . and heard its sweet-sounding, victorious snap.

The crowd continued to roar and stamp its approval. Record or no record, that was a race.

Gil slowed to a stop, and kept walking. The leg man for a national radio broadcast asked Gil to say a few words over the air. He gasped out,

"I thank the Lord for guiding me through this race and once more seeing fit to let me win. I thank Him always for His guiding presence."

Finished, he went back to the track and kept on walking until he regained his normal breath. He reached his sweat suit, picked it up and put it on. By this time the clocks of the four judges had been compared and the announcer walked to the microphone.

"The winner — Gil Dodds, Boston Athletic Association.

"The time — a new world's record . . . 4:06.4 minutes . . ."

and his voice was smothered as the crowd set up another roaring cheer and applauded the stocky, well-built man with glasses. Several of Gil's competitors came over, shook his hand and slapped him on the shoulder. Pictures were snapped. The crowd melted away, and Gil was free to find his way slowly to the locker room.

There the supple hands of a trainer plied him back to normality. Into his street clothes, with occasions here and there for congratulations and autographs as someone managed to slip by the doorman.

Out to the Arena where officials of the meet, sponsored by the Chicago Daily News, asked him to say a few words. The crowd subdued its cheer as the microphone was placed in his hand. Gil Dodds started to talk.

"I appreciate your kindness to me," he said, "and I think that many of you know and realize that running is only a hobby with me. My main job is serving the Lord Jesus Christ, and it was only through prayer that a world's record was set tonight. Thank you, and good night."

Silence for a moment, as the meaning of those words dug themselves into many a heart and mind. Then the cheers rolled again. Out through a door went Gil Dodds, there to be besieged by hundreds of autograph-seekers, each one in turn getting the famous name, "Gil Dodds," with a Bible verse tacked onto it.

* * *

That, in brief, tells you of two nights in the life of Gil Dodds, the world's greatest indoor miler as of 1944 and unbeatable on the indoor track.

It brings to you two looks at the 1943 winner of the Sullivan award as the "amateur athlete who had done the most to advance the cause of sportsmanship during the year."

It shows you a track ace who of a certainty would have been a great Olympic hero had not World War II come along. It reveals the man who gave Sweden's great Gunder Hagg all of the competition he could ask for in the summer of 1943.

Truly, one of the greatest distance runners in all history!

His records are innumerable, his trophies and medals hard to get into one little apartment in Boston, his press notices the best and most friendly of any athlete in many, many years, his "Scripture-quoting" and Bible-verse autograph making him internationally known, his principle of never running a race on Sunday absolutely unbroken on his way to the top, his giving of the credit for all of his triumphs to the Lord Jesus Christ, his complete dependence on prayer, his willingness to sacrifice a chance to defend a national title to preach a sermon in a small church in Indiana—add them all up, mix well with a pleasing personality and a fine sense of humor and you get a composite picture of Gil Dodds, who says "I run for Christ."

Chapter II

A STONE . . . A LADY . . . A DECISION

The 13-year-old boy, bubbling with energy, sat fidgeting in a youth evangelism class. This wasn't his first appearance in the class, nor was it his first time when the "Bible" and "salvation" had been explained to him.

He knew in his mind, at least, most of the things which the lady in charge was explaining. Because he knew, there was a battle going on in the heart of the lad. This "puzzle" had him up in the air for sure.

Through his mind raced the pranks of the past few weeks. The one that stood out forcefully was the instance when, on his way home from fishing with some of his pals, he had picked up a rock and tossed it at the car of a passing farmer.

The brakes had screeched. The guilty-conscienced lad went speedily over a hill with a husky farmer in fast pursuit. The boy thought he could out-run the farmer, but it wasn't long before a hand grabbed at a jacket, a panting boy stopped and the foot of a farmer planted a kick in its proper place.

The boy had come back to his snickering playmates and asked,

"Who was that guy?"

And they told him,

"Lloyd Hahn."

Lloyd Hahn! The name electrified the little fellow when first he heard it. Everyone knew about Lloyd Hahn, and now he had met the famous Hahn, even though the meeting was painful. In the little town of

Falls City, Neb., near which this scene took place and near which Lloyd Hahn had his farm, the former Olympic games hero was as popular as anyone to the idolizing youngsters. Holder of five indoor world records at one time from 1924-1929, the fame and name of Lloyd Hahn still was felt though this was years later.

Thoughts of that prank criss-crossed in the mind of the little "rock-thrower." Ever since he could remember, he had had a desire to be a runner, to race and to compete in track meets.

Meeting this desire broadsides was an equally deep desire to be a Christian such as those about whom his father preached from Sunday to Sunday in a Falls City church.

"But can I be both?" he reasoned. In his little mind he thought he couldn't. Well-meaning friends had said, "You can't be a Christian and an athlete at the same time." Sensitive ears had picked those words up and a mind mulled them over and over.

But this day was different!

The lady talking knew whereof she spoke, and God was using the Bible that day to drive home point after point to convince an eager youth of his need of salvation. Finally a verse which seemed completely directed at him only came from her lips,

"But they that wait upon the Lord shall renew their strength; they shall mount up with wings as eagles; they shall run, and not be weary; and they shall walk, and not faint." Isaiah 40:31.

Then and there God spoke to that little fellow through that verse. At once his doubts about being a Christian and an athlete at the same time disappeared. On that day, when only 13 years of age, Gil Dodds, a "preacher's kid" who was destined to become one of the greatest milers of all time, gave his heart and life to the Lord Jesus Christ, coming to the realization, as he himself explained it, that "Ye must be born again."

The lady leading the class was God-given Mrs. N. C. Hays. It was through her gentle counselling, too, that Gil Dodds realized that same day that there was but one place for him in this world—the ministry. Ever since that day his deep desire to be a runner has stayed with him and been fulfilled to a great extent, but through and above it all, motivating him at all times, has been a desire to be a preacher

Where the two have clashed, the miler has taken second place and the minister has stepped to the fore.

* * *

Gil Dodds was no "unusual child." He grew up just like the rest of us.

He was born on June 23, 1918, at Norcatur, Kansas, the son of Rev. and Mrs. J. G. Dodds. Gil's father was a minister of the Gospel in the First Brethren church and at this time was serving the church at Reiger, Kansas. Gil is one of five children, and was the first to bless the Dodds home.

Later came the following: *Bertha Lee*, born at Morton Grove Mo.; *Myron "Mike"* born at Falls City, Neb.; *Nadine*, born at Shickly, Neb., and *Marilyn*, born at Falls City, Neb.

Gil's father was half English and half Irish and his mother was 100 per cent German. They comprise one of the ideal and model families in American life and the type of family from which many of our great men have come. It was a fine Christian home, in which the Word of God was read, revered, and respected at all times.

Of his family, home, and parents Gil once told a

Acme

A world's record snaps at Chicago Stadium on March 18, 1944.
Time: 4:06.4 minutes.

Two steps behind Gunder Hagg at Camp Randall, N. Y.

Acme

PICTURE

PARADE

Courtesy of Ashland Times Gazette

Trainer George Donges of Ashland College with Gil and Erma after first national title.

Gil the trapper. A collegiate record is broken

Spreadeagling field to win 1936 Nebraska state half-mile championship in 2:01.8 minutes.

The family: left to right, Gil, Myron, Valerie, Gil's mother, Marilyn (in front) Bertha Lee, Pastor Dodds, Erma.

Bill McKee, Gil's "Boswell."

Father and son in the pulpit.   P. A. Inc.   At Sampson Naval Training Station.   U. S. Navy Official Photo

With Jack Wyrtzen in Madison Square Garden.   Torrey Johnson interviews Gil at Chicago Stadium Rally.

The "second coach" passes the food.

Jackie learns to walk.

Gil studies, flanked by trophy array.   "A cup of this, two of that . . . ."

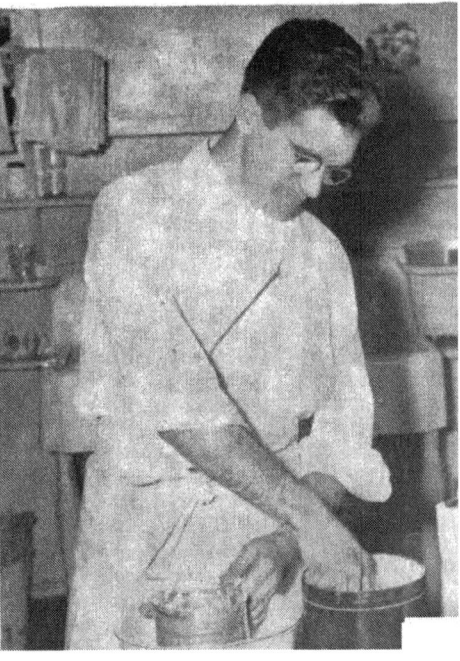

Right at home with the boys in Erie, Pa., YMCA.

Jack Ryder, maker of champions.

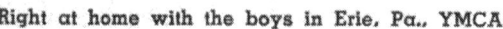

Symmetry of motion! Hagg trails Gil at mile mark in Los Angeles two-mile race

Acme

Above: Gil and Lloyd Hahn examine a shoe.   P. A. I
Below: With Glenn Wagner, and Peter Boyko at Fort Bragg, N. C.
(U. S. Signal Corps Photo)
Arms encircling are Gil, Gunder Hagg and Bill Hulse.

Receiving the famed Sullivan trophy from L. di Benedetto, president of the Amateur Athletic Union.
(P. A. Inc.)

Lt. Comm. John J. O'Donnell presents Spellman trophy after setting world's record in New York.
Acme

The champ's smile and the Bankers' Mile trophy. (Chicago Daily News Photo)

newspaper reporter, "Dad and Mother have helped me along at all times. Even before I became a Christian they shaped and formed my thinking as regards the Bible and the great truths therein. Since my acceptance of Christ they have greatly shaped my theology on many questions."

Gil was, perhaps, the usual "preacher's kid" when it came to having fun and playing pranks. He still has that fine sense of humor and it helps him immensely as he proves to non-Christians how truly happy one can be as a Christian. "The "stone-throwing incident" had its likes in other ways of fooling around, but even through the pranks there moved a seriousness that indicated that he was going places. This was especially true after he accepted the Lord as his Saviour.

Though track has been the topmost hobby in his life he hasn't allowed it to make him lopsided. His early years were well-rounded, and even after he started to run he kept up his interests in many other lines. To accomplish some of the things he desired he worked his way through high school by carrying papers, by doing odd jobs, and by trapping. He was interested in everything, and everything interested him.

Up until he was 13 years old the idea and dream of being a great distance runner was mainly a "castle in the air" for Gil Dodds. He literally dreamed of "some day sinking my spikes into Madison Square Garden's pine track". When things straightened themselves out in his mind and heart when he was 13, he started to work to that end.

Gil often has said, "You don't need to be the best to succeed," and he proves his case by citing his own example. He was just a kid who liked to run. When he started to run he bought all of his own track equipment from his hard-earned money; in fact, he did this all through high school and through two years of college. Once he started to work for his goal, however, Gil really worked. A sports writer in New York, after watching one of Gil's man-killing training drills, wrote, "He may depend on the Lord for his strength, but he sure believes in doing his bit to get into shape during the week."

Gil started to run all alone.

No other young fellows in Falls City wanted to run nor showed any inclination to run. So, he ran alone . . . and liked it.

He found plenty of reasons for running, too. A friend, Bob Kimmel, did a good deal of trapping in and near Falls City and Gil was his buddy on many of those excursions. Gil then conceived the idea of operating a trap line, and after it was operating, it was found to have only one drawback. Even by getting up at the crack of dawn Gil couldn't get around to his various lines, make it home to breakfast and then to school in time. The solution: run between the traps. And so if you had been out on the plains of Nebraska a few years back as dawn did its awakening you might have seen a boy loping from trap to trap checking the lines at the same time as he built up a strong pair of legs and a good deal of stamina.

That took him some 12 miles each day. Added to that was his newspaper route, upon which his customers soon ceased to be surprised when they saw their paperboy running up to the house as though their copy held the "hottest" story in years.

Not far from the Dodds home was a lake which performed double duty for Gil. He liked to swim, so he swam there. In off seasons it also served as a convenient thing around which to run and gave him a chance to time himself and note improvement.

One of the stories that brings out the humorous side of Gil Dodds reverts back to his early days of running. His dad liked to hunt and in Nebraska the jackrabbits were more than plentiful. When his dad went out to hunt , Gil once jokingly told a crowd of 3,000 people at a summer conference grounds, "he didn't want to shoot just the skinny rabbits so he had me run alongside of them and tickle their sides to see if they were fat enough to shoot at. If they were fat enough I'd wave to Dad and he would shoot."

Then Gil would smile and say, "I only wish I could run as fast as a jackrabbit. The four-minute mile would be easy then."

The Dodds home at Falls City was quite a distance from the high school, which presented another problem. Around noon Gil, being normal, would get hungry. If he walked home and back he would be late for afternoon classes. The solution—run both ways. And so every noon as soon as the last bell had rung Gil would start scooting for home. There he would eat a good meal, rest a few minutes to let the food settle and then run back to school to slip into his seat just before the afternoon class bell would do its work.

But now we're in high school.

Chapter III

HIGH SCHOOL ... HAHN ... HONORS

JIMMY Ramsey, a likable sports writer in Falls City, Neb., was talking.

"Mr. Hahn, I'd like to have you meet Gil Dodds. Gil this is Lloyd Hahn. I understand you've 'sort of' met before, if I'm not mistaken."

They had met before, though under different circumstances. The first time a kick had been well placed. This time they shook hands, Gil awkwardly and self conscious, and Hahn the picture of ease and helpfulness.

Gil Dodds had run a race and won it and local high school fans were getting steamed up about the quiet "preacher's kid." Jimmy Ramsey did the preliminary work, Gil Dodds met Lloyd Hahn ... and, on his way was another world champion!

To many of us the name of Lloyd Hahn is but a memory. Sport page readers remember him well, however. It would be hard for them to forget. When Hahn was in his prime from 1924 through 1929 he set five world's records. He chalked up marks in the 880 (a sensational 1:51.2 minutes), the 800 meters, 1,000 meters, 1,500 meters, and three-quarter mile. He had gone to Boston in 1924, reported to Jack Ryder, veteran Boston Athletic Association coach, and said,

"Mr. Ryder, my name is Hahn. Lloyd Hahn. Will you teach me how to run?"

Jack Ryder, who a few years later was to coach another Nebraskan named Gil Dodds, said,

"Sure, son, come on."

And Lloyd Hahn came on . . . to set world's records and become one of America's top heroes in the 1924 and 1928 Olympics.

After he finished racing, Hahn retired to his beloved Nebraska plains to set up farming near Falls City. A fine Christian man, he has been an ideal coach to Gil Dodds. Observers have been led to wonder just why Hahn should have his farm near Falls City and why, too, Rev. J. G. Dodds should accept the call to the Falls City Brethren church, bringing along with him a little lad who was interested in one main thing outside of the church—running. To Christians the answer is obvious. Lloyd Hahn possessed some running information to impart to Gil Dodds which would enable Gil to do more for the Lord Jesus Christ on the track.

When Hahn was asked to help Gil with a few tips, he readily agreed. He didn't travel to town every day to coach Gil, but he was in often enough to keep tab on the promising prepster. Perhaps even more than as a coach, Hahn inspired Gil by his Christian life. Gil could see in Hahn that an athlete could be an athlete and a Christian at the same time. Hahn had proved it before and he was proving it now as he served as a deacon in his church and the Sunday School teacher of a large men's class. Hahn recognized Christ's power and guiding in his life.

But we're ahead of our story. Soft-spoken Gil Dodds probably never would have asked Lloyd Hahn to coach him at any time, but two races in which he participated all by himself brought him into the news and into the limelight, in which he has been basking, to the glory of the Lord, for many years.

In 1935 Gil heard of a track meet at Peru, Nebraska.

That wasn't far away but in his working on odd jobs, newspaper route, trapping, etc., Gil hadn't quite been able to save up enough money to make the trip. He talked it over with his mother and she said that she would rather not have him go but that if he wanted to go it was all right if he could pay his own way.

Gil checked with his school authorities and they had no objections to his going. He had purchased his own track shoes and had "remodeled" some of his underwear, so he was ready. After counting out all of his money, he climbed on the bus. He rode as far as his money lasted and got off. Then his thumb went into action and he hitch-hiked the rest of the way.

Upon arriving, Gil looked up the necessary Southeastern conference officials, explained where he was from, that he had come alone because Falls City had no track coach or team, and that he wanted to run. The officials did the necessary checking and he was entered in two races—the mile and the half mile.

Then he proceeded to be the outstanding athlete of the meet!

He set a new record in the mile, lowering the old mark to 4:49.6 minutes, 13.4 seconds under the former mark. He ran the half-mile in 2:09.5 minutes, breaking the old standard by 4.5 seconds.

The next day the Falls city *Journal* had these words:

"Perhaps the most interesting thing in the meet, of concern to Falls City, was the discovery of Gilbert Dodds, a sophomore who ran the mile and half mile. He had no basic training whatsoever and it was not learned until the day of the meet that he could run."

Following this feat sports writer Ramsey did his introducing work.

In one of his earlier races, when he was a freshman,

Gil had quite an experience. He hitch-hiked to a meet and on arriving in the morning decided to do what he had heard older athletes talk about. They had said you needed *strength* to finish those races so Gil sat down and spent some of his hard-earned money by filling himself up on pancakes. Whatever else, he thought, he was going to have plenty of strength for this race.

Around noon he remembered how they had said, "Eat plenty of meat to build up stamina." This prompted Gil to move to a hot dog stand where he consumed eight hot dogs. His money was going down, but he had to be set for that race!

The race started, and so did Gil. All went well for a few laps and then he started to get a sideache. He thought it would pass over in a few seconds but the pain increased instead of getting better. He slowed down and everyone went past him. Finally he pulled over to the side of the track, stepped off, saw an inviting and shady tree a little bit away and lay under it for the rest of the meet. That was his first lesson in what kind of food to eat to be an athlete.

After Hahn had seen him run he was deeply impressed with his possibilities. Gil had that "easy running" style and gave the appearance of relaxing as he ran. One fault was corrected immediately—he was landing on his heels and not on his toes on every stride. Through the spring of his sophomore year most of Gil's coaching help came from his sports-minded father and from a thorough study of his own running ability and the faults he himself felt he had to correct.

The state track meet loomed on the horizon and Gil was entered in the mile. A year before, as a freshman, he had staggered across fourth in the mile event and second in the half mile. But now he was "set" for the meet and won the state title in a time of 4:39 minutes. A new rule that year confined him to participating in but one event in the state meet. All of that sophomore year Gil had been Falls City's one-man track and a special convocation in the spring honored him and presented him with his athletic letter.

All next winter Gil ran home from school at noon and at night. He participated in other sports, was active at school and kept saving his money for expenses which he might meet when the track season came along.

When he was a junior Hahn really started to take hold of Gil's training. As a rule, Gil practiced alone. Falls City had dropped track for spring football practice and this prevented Head Coach "Jug" Brown from giving any extended attention to Gil. Falls City had no cinder track so Gil practiced in a pasture. The pasture and the pond around which he ran were his two training sites and cinder tracks were his only when meets came around.

Hahn told Gil to specialize in the half mile. He felt that Gil needed speed in order to become a truly great miler and so they worked on the shorter distance. Gil was unbeaten in dual meets all season and was aiming for a new record in the state meet at Lincoln. It eluded him, however, when he raced the distance in 2:01.8 minutes, failing to break the standing record of 2:00.7 minutes as he fought a heavy wind during the race.

Summer, autumn, and winter passed by again without any regular competition but with Gil staying in good physical condition through participating in other sports and operating his trap line, carrying his newspapers, etc. When hs senior year arrived Gil was at his high school peak. Coach Brown again was tied up with the football team most of the time so Gil drilled alone except for the days when Hahn came in from the farm. He won all of his races preparatory to the State meet at Lincoln and this year Hahn thought it best to run him in the mile.

That race proved to be almost as thrilling as fiction.

Another Nebraska prep ace, Delman Moore of Bartley, had been burning up the records in his section even as Gil had been doing in his. Prospects for a top-notch race in the state tournament were all there. Newspapers played the race up for weeks. Falls City rooters even went so far as to put up $100 that Gil would win, but the Bartley fans declined it by saying that it was bad ethics to bet on a race, but "Oherwise we'd make those Falls City guys wear their felt hats all summer."

Before the race started Gil told reporters, "I'm going to run just like Lloyd Hahn said." And he did just that!

After 100 yards of the race *Gil was last*. The track was fast but a strong wind was working against the possibility of anyone's setting a new record. Soon Gil started to move up. He passed one runner after the other and took the lead. Then he *really* put on the steam. When he finished he was 80 yards ahead of Moore and had broken the state record for the mile by over four seconds! His time was 4:28.1 minutes and the record still stands as of this writing. Falls City fans, some of whom had come to Lincoln for the meet, were jubilant at Gil's triumph.

That race ended Gil's prep career. He had been entered in ten official races and had won all ten of them. In doing so he had set five records—the Southeastern Nebraska half mile in 2:09.5 minutes when a sophomore, the "MINK" half mile when a junior in 2:03 minutes, the Southeastern conference mile when a senior in 4:40.8 minutes, the Beatrice Invitational half mile when a senior in 2:01.7 minutes and the state meet mile record in 4:28.1 minutes.

Where to from here?

Gil hoped to go to the state university of Nebraska at Lincoln. As far as track was concerned he knew he could receive excellent coaching there. His father, however, had been graduated from Ashland college in Ashland, Ohio, in 1914, and he was of the opinion that Gil too should receive his college degree from the school sponsored and operated by the First Brethren denomination. The school had no track team, no track coach, nor was its size—300 students—able to put it in much of an athletic limelight. These thoughts raced through Gil's mind as he was making his decision, but in the fall of 1937 he entered Ashland college.

High school days were over. Falls City days were over, too, it appeared, as his father had accepted the call to a Mexico, Ind., pastorate. But Gil had met someone in Falls City who was slated to have much to do with his future life. Pretty Erma Louise Seeger, a fine Christian daughter of an equally fine Christian family, was a junior in the Falls City high school. Gil conveniently found two jobs that summer in Falls City—in Schoff's Bakery and in the public library.

The summer ended, and four years of college started.

Chapter IV

COLLEGE ... CRISIS ... CUPS ... CHAMPIONSHIPS

ASHLAND College never has been widely known for its athletic teams. Competition is held in many sports but the size of the school precluded any possibility of national recognition.

That is, until Gil Dodds came along.

The school numbers in an average school year 300 students. When Gil arrived in the fall of 1937 it had no track team. Gil had known this and in looking ahead he had gone to Lloyd Hahn and had asked him to do something he had never even heard of before—coach him by mail!

Hahn agreed, and thus through four years of college the team of Hahn-the-Coach and Dodds-the-Runner worked and worked toward keeping the runner up toward the top of the track parade. Sportswriters soon tabbed him as the "Mail Order Miler" and the "Correspondence School runner." But the mail between Ashland and Falls City kept going and coming, and Gil Dodds kept on winning races.

As a freshman Gil met his first defeat.

Invited to the Mansfield Relays at Mansfield, Ohio, in the spring of his freshman year, "Twinkle Toes," as the Ashland collegians came to call him, ran the half mile in two minutes flat but lost to flashy Les Eisenhart of Columbus, who did it in 1:59 minutes. He competed in the Cleveland Athletic Club's annual meet that same spring and won two races. By this time Hahn again felt definitely that the mile was Gil's best race and arranged his training schedule accordingly.

As a sophomore Gil tried cross country running for the first time. He had run many long distances in training but this was the first time he entered any official races. This brought out one of the dominant traits in Gil Dodds' personality. He is extremely enthusiastic about anything he goes into, and cross country is no exception. Hahn was greatly in favor of the idea, too, and in a short while the weekly letter from Falls City was carrying the proper instructions for hill and dale running.

Gil clicked right away in cross country running. In his first year he set a state conference record of 22:02.6 minutes over a 3⅞ mile course, breaking the former mark by 33.4 seconds! That came, too, on his first look at the racing course and while he was working nights. Still he finished 400 yards ahead in winning.

That victory brings into our picture a sports writer who has had much to do with placing Gil Dodds in the national limelight. Sometimes it takes a sports writer or sports editor to beat the publicity drums loud enough so fans outside a local territory will know about a home town favorite. This was true in Dodds' case.

Bill McKee, sports editor of the Ashland *Times Gazette*, had been one of Gil's staunchest supporters ever since he enrolled at Ashland. Knowing and feeling that Gil had the stuff, McKee went all-out for him. Through his efforts Gil was invited to compete in the Sugar Bowl race at New Orleans on January 1, 1939, and it was through his efforts, too, that Gil ever reached New Orleans to race.

The Ashland athletic budget wasn't made to send its teams and athletes all over the country, and consequently after the invitation to the Sugar Bowl event had been received it appeared that Gil would have to refuse because of lack of expense money. Gil was working his way through college by bell hopping at Ashland's Hotel Otter and couldn't afford to pay his own way.

So McKee helped to arrange and sponsor an exhibition basketball game which coughed up the necessary expense money. The game was a success as hundreds of fans did their bit to send their newest athletic star on his way to the top. Ashland college has meant much to Gil Dodds, and the fine spirit of cooperation at that time and at later instances has given him a deep love for the school whose 300 students form "one big, happy family."

To New Orleans went Gil Dodds and into big-time track stepped another star for the first time. His first attempt in Big Time competition came in the Sugar Bowl on January 1, 1939, and although Gil didn't win that race and although he didn't reach the top immediately following that race, he is there now.

Gil was entered in the two-mile race against Don Lash, great University of Indiana runner. It was the first competitive two-mile race that Gil ever had run. When the gun went off Gil swung into his steady, pleasing-to-watch lope. Lap after lap he stayed ahead of Lash. In the middle of the race he lengthened and lengthened that lead. With one lap to go Gil was ahead by 30 yards.

Then the Indiana star started to close the gap. It narrowed slowly because Gil was still running well though very tired. Would he catch "the unknown?" He did, but by only one yard in what proved to be the best race of the entire meet. Lash's time was 9:23.3 minutes and after he had gotten his wind back he told reporters, "The kid had me scared!"

When Gil went home from New Orleans he had in

his pocket an invitation to compete in the famed Millrose games in Madison Square Garden the following month.

Madison Square Garden! A dream coming true! Actually invited to race in the Garden! Gil was thrilled. He went home, drilled intensely for a month and then was off to Madison Square Garden and the Millrose games.

Gil reached New York and his remark at seeing crowded Times Square jammed with people ranks with the best of remarks of people getting their first look at New York. The small Nebraskan, getting his first look at Gotham, blurted out,

"Say, what's going on here. It looks like Saturday."

It was Saturday a few days later when Gil ran in Madison Square Garden for the first time. He had everything to look forward to, everything to plan for, a future in track that looked extremely promising, three years of collegiate racing ahead of him, one of the best coaches in the world training him, etc.

And then the roof fell in and the bottom fell out.

Gil Dodds proved such a flop in his first race in Madison Square Garden that the crowd actually stood up and booed him, calling at him, "Get off the track, you bum!"

Here's how it happened.

Gil was entered in the two-mile race against Greg Rice and Don Lash. The Garden was filled with smoke and this was the first time Gil ever had run in a smoke-filled arena. He started out all right, but began to falter after the half-way mark. Rice lapped him. Gil was having a hard time staying on his feet. Sportswriters have described him as "weaving all over the track, like a drunk."

But his fighting heart wouldn't let him quit. He kept on running, his foot hitting against the curb of the track on almost every stride. Lash was coming up, fast in pursuit of Rice. But he couldn't get past Gil as he wove from side to side and just as he did get by, Gil's foot hit the curb again and he was thrown into Lash.

Lash's stride was broken, but he managed to stay on his feet and went on to trail Rice to the tape. Gil fell to the track as the crowd roared angrily at him for having spoiled the race between Rice and Lash. He picked himself up and walked with head down off the track as boos and catcalls resounded in his ears.

New York newspapers the next day were anything but kind to him. The "mail order" and "correspondence school" remarks were unearthed and tagged onto him for not knowing how to run in big time and for spoiling the cracker jack race between Rice and Lash.

The following week-end Gil competed in the Boston Athletic Association meet at Boston. The invitation to the meet had come before the Millrose games and although Boston officials felt inclined to withdraw his entry after seeing what happened at New York he was allowed to compete. With many of the fans still remembering what had happened the week before, he came in for numerous jibes even in Boston. In the race he stayed from a half foot to a foot from the curb and finished fourth in the two-mile behind Lash.

A saddened Gil Dodds reached Ashland college after that trip east. From all appearances he had "soured himself" forever with big time track meet officials.

But he kept at it.

He still wrote his weekly letter to Hahn and received one in return. Though discouraged he realized that life was more than running in track meets. He swung into his school work with interest; he took part in school activities readily. His job kept him busy. A typical school day found him working at the hotel from 6 to 10 a.m. Then he hurried to classes, to his afternoon workout, and back to work for a few hours at night. Being a bell hop, he was able to do part of his studying on the job. The hotel manager figured Dodds to be one of his "top drawing cards," as far as attracting trade was concerned. When the snows came Gil would get his workout by taking a snow shovel to the track with him and uncovering a lane or path all around the track. This served as his "warmup," and gave him a "clear track" to use for his real workout.

The next spring found Gil back in competition, a bit shaky after the experience in the Garden but determined to reach the top. He placed second to Rice in the Drake Relays, pushing him to a new national collegiate record of 9:10 minutes. He set a Bix Six conference meet record in the two-mile of 9:47.3 minutes, placed second in the Central Collegiate at Milwaukee, where his father saw him compete for the first time, and was fourth in the National Collegiate Athletic Association (NCAA) two-mile at Los Angeles.

The weekly letters of advice kept coming from Hahn and Gil gave all credit to Hahn for any advances he had made. When school was out that spring Gil went to Falls City to see his sweetheart and practice for the Amateur Athletic Union's annual meet at Lincoln. He was in excellent shape for the meet and was entered in the 10,000 meters (six and a fourth miles) race. A sizzling heat wave gripped the Midwest the day of the meet and with one lap to go Gil was forced out of the meet when his legs gave out. He was leading at the time and appeared to have the victory won.

His fame was spreading, however. From way over in China a friend sent him a clipping from the China Press issue of June 4, 1939. The clipping gave two columns and a picture to the "Scripture-quoting" athlete.

After a summer of working and preaching in churches, Gil was back in school in the fall for his junior year. Ashland was interested in track now and a cross country team was formed to run with Gil. In the first race two of the Ashland runners got lost on the course but still managed to finish ninth and tenth to give the team a victory. Gil set a record in that meet as Ashland defeated Wooster, the state champions.

Gil also won the Ohio conference cross-country title in the meet held at Ashland, aiding the team in winning the conference title. This race was the first in which Ashland students and followers saw him run, as the meet was held at Ashland.

Gil competed in the national cross country meet at Lansing, Mich., and finished eighth. With this in mind and remembering the race he had run at New Orleans the year before, Sugar Bowl officials again invited him to run in New Orleans on New Year's Day. But that day fell on Sunday and in line with a principle which Gil has never broken, he refused the invitation. The action was commended by the local ministerial association in Ashland, but it was a hard decision to make as that race generally decided who would be invited to the Millrose games in New York.

So Gil stayed at home that winter, outside of running in an exhibition race against Taisto Maki of Finland at Cleveland on March 29-30. In the outdoor season he placed second in the two-mile at the Texas Relays, second in the Penn Relays, won the mile and lost the two mile in the Ohio conference meet and placed eighth in the N.C.A.A. two-mile at Minneapolis.

The next summer found him working on a state highway crew to stay in tip-top physical shape. He wanted to be at his best for his senior year and his last chance at collegiate laurels. In the preliminary cross country meets in the fall he broke three out of four meet records in those in which he competed, as he won all four races. He captured the Ohio conference title in 20:47 minutes. In one of the races he finished so far ahead that he was able to take a shower, get dressed and snap a picture of the late finishers!

On November 25, 1940, he became a national champion for the first time when he won the national collegiate cross country championship at East Lansing, Mich. Three days before that race he had received a wire from Hahn which read, "Take it easy—you're trained too fine." So Gil laid off training for three days.

On a heavy and muddy course he not only won the race from the top collegiate runners in the United States but also broke the record by 7/10 of a second. He finished the course in 20:32.2 minutes, a full 36.8 seconds better than his time of a year before when he had finished eighth.

He won by 50 yards over Notre Dame's famous Oliver Hunter, and immediately after the race sent a happy wire to a waiting Falls City farmer, "Ran as directed and won." That triumph did a good deal for Gil Dodds. It gave him the confidence he needed. The nation's top distance runners—130 runners from 22 schools—were on hand for that race and so Gil topped the cream of the crop in his victory. Ever since the Millrose games in 1939 Gil had had a fear of "folding up" in a race and that fear had affected his running right down the line.

But now he was "over the hump" and a national championship was his as he left East Lansing that night. That race has other memories, too, for Gil. It had its humorous angles. One of Gil's teammates lost one of his shoes somewhere on the course and finished barefooted. Another runner in the race broke his ankle during the first half of the rugged course and finished the race without even knowing that he had broken a bone in his ankle. Right after the race a friend of Gil's who had worked with him on the highway crew the summer before claimed some credit for Gil's championship. "Why," he said, "I let him do all of my work last summer so he could stay in shape!"

A cheering campus greeted Dodds when he returned. It was the first national championship which Ashland ever had won in any sport and it brought national publicity to Ashland. Ashland was proud of the fellow who shrugged off the friendly taunts of his classmates for getting so much sleep and for not eating rich foods.

The next spring he won the Texas Relays 3,000 meter crown which had eluded him. He was still going strong on the cross country record which had seen him win eight out of nine races in which he had competed over three years. In the Penn Relays he broke the meet record for the two-mile but found himself second to Fred Wilt of Indiana.

Then came a race which surprised even Hahn.

Gil was invited to the Beloit Relays at Beloit, Wis., and after hitch-hiking to the meet he won the mile in 4:13.7 minutes, a full ten seconds faster than he ever had run the mile in competition. Hahn was surprised because usually a cross country star is better at the longer distances, as two miles and three miles, than he is at the mile. Gil too felt lately that the two-mile race

— 35 —

was his best distance.

That Beloit race was the second fastest collegiate mile of the season. George Donges of Ashland, when he heard the time a few days later said, "Say, you must be 10 seconds off there." As Gil sped around the track that day a little Negro boy in the middle of the back stretch called out to him, "Say there bo', what's wrong with you? You got hot rocks in yo' pants?" Along with the medal for winning the mile Gil was awarded a trophy for being the outstanding athlete of the meet, though people at home didn't know about the latter award for a week or so as Gil didn't mention it.

Later that spring Gil won the Ohio conference two-mile run in 9:31.3 minutes, but failed to break the record. If you'll check the Ohio conference record books today, not once will you see the name of Gil Dodds as holding a conference record. He ran many, many fine races and clearly was the outstanding track star in the conference in many years, but an oddity finds him unable to break a conference record in each of his three years of competition.

In Milwaukee Gil ran the two-mile in the Central Collegiate meet in 9:14.5 minutes to win and set the lowest mark in the country that year. This terminated his regular season but it was NCAA time again and Gil's thoughts were turned toward Palo Alto, Calif. and one final chance at the two-mile championship. However, the Ashland budget again was depleted. To the rescue once more came sports editor Bill McKee of the Ashland Times-Gazette, now known as "Gil Dodds' Boswell." McKee started a fund himself and before the publicity was over 39 people had chipped in to send Gil to Palo Alto.

But Gil didn't win.

— 36 —

He placed third to Fred Wilt of Indiana and Bobby Madrid of Fresno, Calif. His fine showing, however, gave him a place on the All-American track team, the first Ashland athlete in history to be so honored.

The national A. A. U. meet was coming up and it would give Gil a chance to redeem himself. But when Gil found that this race would be held on Sunday, he promptly scratched his entry.

That finished Gil Dodds' collegiate career. He wasn't known as the greatest distance runner in college, and what might have happened had he gone to a school which had a track coach and a track team is purely problematical. As an athlete, however, he had gained the admiration of every competitor. Not many people knew that he himself had bought and paid for every bit of track equipment he used until he was a junior in college. He had missed the personal, face-to-face contact with Lloyd Hahn; the usual deep feeling that develops between a coach and his pupil had been somewhat stifled because of the necessity of their talking to each other through the mail. In cross country Gil had reached the top and was without a peer. In more-publicized track, however, he was just on the fringe of being termed great.

Had his running been the only thing Gil was in college for, he might well have been disappointed. Even though these words have dealt mainly with his track exploits, we should not forget his other achievements in college. Track was his hobby—that and nothing more. His main job was being a Christian and letting other people know what it was to be a Christian.

Together with a fellow student Gil had worked to open two closed churches near Ashland. When they left college the churches were thriving again. He spoke often at other churches in and near Ashland, using his testimony as a runner to bring out the Gospel story. In his class work he had finished with a high average in both of his major lines of study, English and history. He had been active in the Gospel Team work as conducted by the students, interested and occupied in the YMCA work, a member of the "A" club, and other extra-curricular activities.

He had taken all of the honor coming to him with Christian humility. In March of his senior year a school banquet had honored him and the basketball team. Graduation came on fast and college was finished.

What was next?

The problem for the summer was solved when he accepted the pastorate of a church at Fort Scott, Kansas. While there he stayed in shape by means of early morning workouts. When fall arrived he enrolled in the Seminary course at Ashland, not knowing exactly what to do and being somewhat in a puzzle. He kept up with his running, however, and that fall hitch-hiked to the Ohio Amateur Athletic Union's state cross country meet and won it. Then, characteristically enough, he thumbed his way out of town to a place 66 miles away to preach there twice the next day.

Hahn had urged Gil to go east for a year and let Jack Ryder, Lloyd's former coach, take him under his wing. He was confident that Gil could reach the top, but Gil, being of a conservative nature and always wanting to be sure of things, didn't think so. But Hahn was clearly convinced that Gil could succeed so he wrote to both Ryder and Walter Brown, president of the Boston Athletic Association, telling them of Gil's sensational time in the Beloit Relays and of his amazing stamina.

A few days later letters arrived from Ryder and the

Boston Athletic Association, asking Gil and his wife if they were interested in coming east. Gil and his wife answered, "Yes, if it's the Lord's will." Then they prayed very definitely about it. Things gradually closed up for Gil in Ashland and then a letter arrived from Mr. Brown stating that he would pay their expenses to Boston, find Gil a job, take care of them for a couple of weeks and if they liked to stay it would be fine. Otherwise, he would pay their way back to Ashland.

This definite answer to prayer led Gil to withdraw from Ashland Seminary and head for Boston. Another evangelical and spiritual Bible school—Gordon School of Theology and Missions—was located there and Gil planned to enroll there for his seminary training.

Horace Greeley said a few years before, "Go west, young man, go west." Gil Dodds reversed the direction, but he also went up the ladder to world fame and success.

Chapter V

BOSTON . . . JACK RYDER . . . FAME

IT was a cold December day when Gil Dodds walked up to Jack Ryder, "maker of champions," in Boston, handed him a letter written by Lloyd Hahn in Falls City, and said,

"Mr. Ryder, Lloyd Hahn sent me to you. I'd like to learn how to run."

Jack Ryder read the letter, looked at Gil and said to him even as he had said to another Nebraskan years before,

"All right, son."

On arriving in Boston Gil had a job in defense work lined up for him by Mr. Brown, but this was changed and he started to work in a city gymnasium. He wanted to serve a church while going to school, feeling that the Lord wanted him to do that and also to relieve the financial strain. First one church apparently was all set to engage him as its pastor when some small item arose and the church decided that it did not want him.

He applied to another church then without a pastor, and the same thing happened! Some small detail, minor in itself, was enough to keep him from getting the call. It was at that time that Gil decided that the Lord wanted him to run while going to school and that "He preferred that I glorify Him by my running, not my preaching, while going to school."

Ryder had heard of Gil Dodds and had seen him run in the Boston Garden in 1939, the week following Gil's flop in New York. The veteran coach didn't know what to expect when Gil showed up. Without asking for instructions Gil jogged an easy mile, rode the bike, went through a half hour of hard calisthenics, jogged and sprinted a little more, and then, when he had done more drilling in a single day than any athlete Ryder ever had trained, he came over to Ryder and said,

"I'm ready to start now, Mr. Ryder. What do you suggest that I do today?"

Then and there Jack Ryder knew he had a pupil who was willing to work.

And work he did. Ryder toiled day in and day out with Gil, admiring the talent built into the sinewy five foot nine inch frame. The veteran Boston Athletic Association coach, who has developed more track champions than perhaps any other coach, believed in Dodds' greatness from the first. He saw a body whose muscles could absorb unusual punishment. He marvelled at the amazing recuperative powers which Dodds has: two minutes after a gruelling mile race his breathing is back to normal! He saw in Dodds a modern miracle—a man who didn't have a sprint but still a man who could approach the four-minute mark in the mile in race after race.

The explanation lies in Dodds' tremendous stamina. Gil doesn't "save himself" in any race. Once that starting gun goes off he starts running as hard as he can and doesn't quit until the race is over. His new "powerhouse" type of running surprised track experts at first. As a rule a miler would run slower the second and third quarters in a mile race, but Gil is just the opposite. His second and third quarters generally are his best as he "pours it on."

Ryder was amazed at his pacing power. He would tell Gil to run a practice mile in 4:50 minutes. Gil often would hit it right on the nose. That pacing power has proved invaluable to Ryder and to Dodds.

In Jack Ryder Gil found an ideal coach. Lloyd Hahn knew of but one man to send Gil to for further training. That man was Jack Ryder.

Dodds is Ryder's prize exhibit and there exists between the two a deep friendship of mutual love and admiration. Ryder is a very devout Catholic and this has cemented rather than hindered their working together. Whenever Gil would get in a tough race, or lose one, Ryder as often as not would remind Gil, "Now, Gil, don't we say when we pray, 'Thy will be done?'"

In zero weather they drilled together. Ryder risked pneumonia time and time again to be with Gil in those winter drills. Sports writers often have wondered why the venerable Ryder did it. There is no pay connected with his job as coach of the Boston A.A. track team and the time he puts in with his "stable" surely is valuable. Ryder lives for track and Gil's coming to Boston put "new life" into him, allowing him to develop his greatest champion.

Gil almost worshipped Ryder. He followed his orders explicitly and to the letter. He told a sports writer once, "I don't think I'll ever be able to repay Coach Jack Ryder. I have implicit faith in him. I'll always welcome his advice. He's the best coach a man ever had. There's none other like him."

Ryder knows his track and knows his athletes. The sporting scene has known few men who can judge athletes as Ryder has done. At times his predictions for Gil have seemed a bit far fetched but time and time again Gil has come through with triumphs in record times to fulfill his prophecies.

Ryder is a fluent speaker and knows how to write

and speak between nine to 19 languages with varying proficiency. He learned these when working with the immigration department of the Federal government. He also is a good writer, plays the violin and piano, and is justly proud of his record as a champion checker player. He is employed at Boston College, where he serves as track coach and professor of physical education.

When Gil first came east several friends warned him that he never would get anywhere in big time racing because so many of the races were held on Sunday and Gil didn't run on Sundays. Gil's reply was his usual, God-guided answer, "If the Lord sees fit to have me run, He'll make it possible that I won't have to run on Sunday."

This has proved to be the case. Gil never has run in a race on Sunday. To him it is strictly the Lord's day. A few meets have been moved to accommodate him, including two national A.A. U. races which were moved ahead from Sunday to Saturday to allow Gil to run.

Which brings up the story of one such two-day meet. Gil's specialty was scheduled for Saturday and a few minutes before the race was to start a thunderstorm loomed up. One of Gil's opponents jokingly suggested, "Let's pray for rain so they'll postpone the race until tomorrow and then Gil won't run."

But the storm passed over . . . and Gil passed the runners to win the race.

Ryder started to work with Gil in December, 1941. He arranged so Gil could dress in the same locker room as used by Hahn years before, and even use the same locker. Through December and January they drilled together in the cold of the winter. Then Gil was invited to the Millrose games in Madison Square Garden.

Much went through Gil's mind after that invitation

was received. It would be hard to explain his feelings. Three years before he had been booed out of the Garden as the "Get outta there, ya bum!" cries had reached his burning ears.

But, a crowd soon forgets. The promoters needed someone to run against phenomenal Greg Rice and so they took the word of trusty Jack Ryder and invited Gil back for the meet.

It wasn't until three days before the race that he knew he was going to run the two-mile. He had been training for the mile, but when the promoter asked him to run the two-mile in order to provide competition for Rice, he agreed.

Just before the race he received a wire of encouragement from the "old highway crew gang" back in Ohio. Three years before, in this same race in this same meet, Gil Dodds the sophomore in college had folded up completely, had been lapped by Rice and had spoiled the bid of Don Lash to overcome Rice.

But this night it was different.

Gil didn't defeat Rice. He never has done that, although they have had many close races. But about the time in the race when Rice's opponents usually start to lag behind and let him go on to unchallenged victory, an unknown from the Boston A.A. started to give Rice a fight for the lead. Track programs hurriedly were scanned for his number . . . "Gil Dodds, Boston A.A." That finish tape was getting closer, and still the dark-haired runner with glasses didn't fall back. Right up until the last few yards Gil was ahead; then the final, famous Rice "kick" moved him past Gil to win by three yards in the fast time of 8:53.2 minutes.

That lone race revived track interest in the east. Out of nowhere but Jack Ryder's vest pocket had stepped an unknown, a divinity school student who had learned the fundamentals of running through the mail and now was ready to meet anyone on his own footing. Once more Jack Ryder had a champion and once more there was talk of someone beating invincible Greg Rice.

The following week the Boston A.A. games were scheduled for the Boston Garden. The newspapers built up a great Rice-Dodds duel. Rice won decisively this time as Gil didn't do so well before his new "home town folks." He trailed Rice by 50 yards, although even a victory that night would not have meant too much as it was at that meet that Cornelius Warmerdam, the California pole vaulter, sailed over the bar at 15 feet, 7¾ inches for an all-time world record.

The next week it was back to New York for the New York Athletic club meet. Gil almost defeated Rice here again but trailed by three yards at the finish. Seven days later, in the Amateur Athletic Union's national indoor meet, Rice decided to run the three-mile race. Gil didn't think it would be too much fun chasing Rice for three miles so Ryder entered him in the mile. Heavily favored and recognized king of the milers was Les MacMitchell, one of track's all-time greats and sporting a string of 19 straight victories. A few hours before the race he had been awarded the Sullivan trophy for being the outstanding amateur athlete for 1941. Everything pointed to another MacMitchell victory, this to be No. 20.

But Gil Dodds proceeded to spoil a great day for MacMitchell.

Gil ran the mile that day in 4:08.7 minutes for a new national AAU indoor record. He was ahead of MacMitchell all of the way and when the New York ace tried to close the gap by his final sprint Gil was too far out in front and he fell a yard short. This was the greatest upset of the indoor season and stunned the crowd and the sporting world.

That triumph *really* brought Gil up with the cream of the runners. He fulfilled Ryder's predictions and hopes and brought joy to the heart of the Boston College track coach. It brought much-needed confidence to Gil and gave him that assurance that he was just as good as the rest of them. Newspapers the country over filled their columns about the "Scripture-quoting seminary student from Boston."

After the race Gil went on a "spree"—he ate two honey and butter sandwiches and drank a bottle of milk. He startled the well-fortified AAU by presenting an expense account of only $17 for the meet—$10.60 for train fare and $6.40 for board and room. Seventeen dollars! .... after the AAU had been paying expense accounts into the hundreds for other athletes.

But the lickings were still to come. A few weeks later MacMitchell defeated Gil in the Columbia mile in New York. This preceded the annual Chicago Relays sponsored by the Chicago Daily News in which Gil had reverted to the two-mile by request, only to be defeated once again by "Rambling Rice." It was after the Chicago race that Gil's wife said, "Why expend all of that energy chasing someone? Why not compete in the mile and beat MacMitchell?"

So, back to the mile. Gil always has felt that he can run the two-mile better than the mile, but figures have proved him wrong from time to time. At least he can break records in the mile and win races, and this hasn't been true in the two-mile.

MacMitchell's triumph in the Columbian mile left each of them with one victory. The setting was ideal for a final race and it was held for Navy Relief in New York on March 25, 1942. Before that race the promoter had asked Gil which race he would rather run. Gil answered,

"Whichever race will bring the most for Navy Relief. Where's an entry blank?"

They handed him one and he signed it.

"One mile or two-mile."

Gil would run any race that would swell the gate receipts or help along his favorite sport or any service cause. When the plans for the meet were completed they asked him to compete in the mile against Mac-Mitchell. The race was a dandy and MacMitchell won in 4:07.8 minutes, up until that time the fifth fastest mile on record! Gil finished second with 4:08.5 minutes in a race that had the fans on their feet through all of the final laps.

The indoor season was over and as it ended, firmly perched on the throne as the "newcomer of the year" was Gil Dodds of Boston. He almost had defeated Rice three times and he had handed MacMitchell his lone defeat in nine races. When sports writers looked at that long list of second places they quipped, "Often a bridesmaid, but never a bride." It may have been true then, but not for long.

The snows melted, the ground softened up . . . and the outdoor season was here. Gil tuned up for the national A.A.U. meet by winning the New England A. A.U. mile championship in 4:13 minutes, breaking a 29-year old record by six seconds as the old recordholder, Jimmy Powers, looked on. All through the nation the stars were getting set for the top outdoor meet of the season—the national A.A.U. meet. This year it was held on June 20, 1942, in New York. The 1,500 meter race (called the metric mile) was the feature of the two-day tournament and carried in it the greatest field of the year. MacMitchell, of course, was the favorite.

But Dodds came through with a blazing 3:50.2 minutes to win the race, with LeRoy Weed second and MacMitchell third. This was the second time he had defeated MacMitchell and this time it was decisively. From all outward appearances, Gil apparently was on the throne.

That summer he worked in Boston, running in and winning three races and placing second in a handicap three-mile race on July 4 in Boston after winning his first race that day.

When the 1943 indoor season came along everyone expected Dodds to reach his peak. He had trained hard all fall and early winter and apparently was ready for the indoor season. He won some races, but he lost others. This was the winter that sports writers, other track coaches, promoters and well-meaning friends tried to help Jack Ryder in coaching Gil. It also was the year that Frank Dixon, New York university freshman, was on his way up, and Bill Hulse, New York research analyst, also was challenging. Gil won more than his share of the races, including the famed Bankers' Mile in the Chicago Relays, and when the season was over he had more firsts than either Dixon or Hulse. As a whole, however, the season hadn't been the standout to which he and Jack Ryder had looked forward. At the A.A.U. outdoor meet he again proved his supremacy by winning the 1,500 meter race and lowering his time of a year previous to 3:50 minutes. He was the undoubted "king of the milers," but not the undefeated king.

But this was summer, 1943, and to America from

Sweden came long-legged, amiable Gunder Hagg, the great Swedish runner. Hagg needed competition and needed it badly after Greg Rice moved into the maritime service. There was no one to push the Swedish star to hoped-for records, so the A.A.U. asked Gil to compete against him all over the country.

Gil agreed, and that led to further glory.

Chapter VI

HAGG ... SULLIVAN AWARD ... WORLD RECORD!

THE first race in which Gunder Hagg competed in the United States was held on a Sunday. The race had been scheduled in advance and when the Swedish freighter on which he traveled arrived at New Orleans, only a few days before the race, efforts were made to postpone or cancel the meet. However, officials decided to go through with it.

Hagg wasn't in tip-top shape and still had his sea legs even though he had been able to train a little since reaching America. Greg Rice was out of shape, being in the maritime service, and had Gil accepted the invitation to run against Hagg and Rice that Sunday he easily might have achieved world-wide fame by defeating Hagg and Rice.

But once more he chose not to run on Sunday. Hagg won the race, Greg Rice returned to the service and the sponsoring A. A. U. was stuck without a distance competitor for Hagg and his races in the United States.

Gil had planned to work all summer to make the necessary money to put himself through school the next year. When the A.A.U. asked Gil to make the tour with Hagg it meant the loss of his "financial summer." But he consented readily: he always has done his best to further the cause of track and he was anxious to say yes to their request inasmuch as all proceeds were to go to the Army Air Force Aid Society.

Seven times Gil raced against Hagg ... and seven

times he trailed him across the finishing line. As he told one audience, "I chased him around the track so much and so often that by the end of the summer I could tell you the exact number of stitches in the seat of his pants."

If Hagg and the promoters wanted to race two miles they raced two miles. If it was one mile they raced one mile. This led Gil to use yet another verse of Scripture when, in being told that the race in Chicago would be two miles he quoted Matthew 5:14, "And whosoever forces thee to go a mile, go with him twain."

There grew up between these two great runners a fine, deep friendship. Sportswriter's tabbed Hagg "Gunder the Wonder" soon after he landed, and in many ways he was a wonder. Gil spoke to Hagg often on their cross country tour, usually through an interpreter, although by the end of the summer they could dispense with the interpreter as Hagg had picked up English fast after arriving.

Gil admired Hagg for his dependence upon the Lord in his running. Before every race Hagg spent a definite time in speaking to and communing with God, or the "Supreme Being", as he referred to God. In one race a slight delay held things up for a few moments. Gil noticed Hagg's lips moving and through his interpreter he told Gil, "I just prayed to God that He would let each one of us do his best in this race." Gil always found that the runners hardest to defeat are the ones who believe in prayer—Greg Rice is another—and Hagg proved to be no exception.

Anyone who saw Hagg run that summer was impressed by his greatness. He won every race and the competition was the best in America. He truly is a great runner, not only in the eyes of the sport world but also in the eyes of his competitors. When Gil finished the summer he had this to say: "I thank God for the strength that enabled me even to stay close to this great runner."

Hagg liked his sleep. Some nights he would sleep the clock around. Before the race in Chicago he slept from 11 p.m. Friday to 11 a.m. Saturday. Then he got up, did a few limbering up exercises ... ate a little ... and went back to sleep!

One day he would eat two meals. The next day he would eat four. He liked milk shakes, but not plain ice cream. He insisted that Gil warm up first so that he could run behind him as they circled the track. He took the filling out of pies and ate only the crust. Gil says that he is one of the most carefree persons he has ever met.

On his left wrist he wore a gold bracelet which he regarded as a good luck charm and would not run without it. It was a gift from a girl in Sweden. He thought that Gil's shoes weighed too much and promised to send him three pairs of the lighter, Swedish type, with longer spikes, when he reached home. After they had finished the tour he took one of his shoes and wrote on it in Swedish as follows:

"To my good friend Gil Dodds for much track and good running and good companionship. Welcome to Sweden some day. May God give you happiness and fame in your chosen profession, the ministry. Your friend for life. Gunder Hagg."

The depth of their friendship was shown when Christmas, 1943, came along. On Christmas morning a cablegram from Sweden arrived at the Dodds apartment in Boston, wishing the Dodds family a Merry Christmas from Gunder Hagg. Gil was pleasantly surprised to get it and asked Coach Ryder, "Why would he do such a swell thing for me, Jack?"

Races were held in Chicago, Los Angeles, San Francisco, Boston, Berea, Ohio, Cincinnati, and New York. The race in Boston proved to be the highlight of the entire tour. Up until this time Gil never had been able to run well before his Boston admirers. For some reason or other his best races were run on distant tracks. This day, however, it was different, even though Hagg again won the race.

It was in this race that Gil forced Hagg to run his best race of the summer and set a new all-time mile record for the United States. Th Swedish star ran the distance in 4:05.3 minutes, Gil trailing in second place with 4:06.5 minutes, up until that time the fastest mile any American ever had run. Finishing third was Bill Hulse with 4:07.8 minutes. Although Hagg won the race, Gil firmly established himself as the greatest miler America ever has known by breaking the American mark held by Glenn Cunningham of Kansas.

When he had reached Boston a week before that race, Gil was far from being in top shape. He was tired from the trip. On the long jaunt he had been forced to sleep in an upper berth while Hagg had a compartment. Often he couldn't get a trainer when he wanted one. Had the A.A.U. offered to send Jack Ryder along with him on the trip there might have been a difference in results. When he reported back to Ryder in Boston he had lost several pounds and was strained and tired. After a week of rest and treatment under Ryder he had gained back part of his weight and was almost in shape to test Hagg. Though he didn't win he gave Hagg the greatest scare of the summer.

The last race was held in New York and proved to

be an anti-climax. The week before, Hagg had run the mile in 4:05.4 minutes in Cincinnati as Bill Hulse blazed through with a 4:06 minute mile to supplant Gil's 4:06.5 of the Boston meet as the fastest American mile ever run in competition. In the finale, Hagg slipped to 4:06.9 minutes and still managed to win as Gil trailed with 4:07.2 minutes.

The summer was over and it had been a pleasant and profitable one in many ways. The crowds contributed $136,000 to the Army Air Force Relief Fund to see these two champions meet. All across the country Gil had left a stream of Bible-versed autographs. In San Francisco he gave his testimony over the radio on a special broadcast. The day after the Boston race he was in Worcester, Mass., speaking in three services. He presented a true picture of a Christian gentleman on that entire tour. Fans flocked to see Hagg . . . and to see Dodds chase Hagg.

Gil had sacrificed much that summer. His financial summer was gone, and not once did he pad his expense account. On one trip, for example, he charged the A.A.U. $12.01 for a round trip ticket from Boston to New York. That represented the exact cost of the ticket; he didn't even charge them for the food he ate on the train. These minor things endeared him to fans and officials all over the country. He always praised Hagg; not once did he complain of a thing on the trip. The complaints usually were lodged by reporters who noticed how things were being run. Gil just ran and ran and ran. Sometimes it was one mile; sometimes it was two. He was licked every time, but he kept on coming back.

Add all of these little items together and you get the reason why in December of 1943 the Amateur Athletic Union bestowed on Gil Dodds the greatest honor that can be given to any amateur athlete in the United States — the prized, sought-for, dreamed-of Sullivan award, given annually to the amateur athlete in the United States who has done the most to further the cause of sportsmanship during the year.

Winner of the Sullivan award!

Gil hardly could believe Jack Ryder when he told him. He sincerely asked Ryder, "Do you really think it's true, Jack?" and Jack told him it was.

Never has more sincere and fulsome praise been poured out on the Sullivan award winner than when Gil was announced as the winner. Given in memory of a founder of the A.A.U., the award is the dream of every amateur athlete. Gil had stood next to Don Lash on January 1, 1939, between halves of the Texas Christian-Carnegie Tech football game in the Sugar Bowl when Lash received the award for the previous year. He remarked later to George Donges, attending with Gil from Ashland college as Gil competed in the two-mile, "I'd rather have the Sullivan award than anything else."

Four years later it was his.

The Sullivan award winner is selected in the following manner: Each of the 41 districts of the A.A.U. nominates a candidate for the honor and a committee then picks 10 of those nominees. These ten names are submitted to 600 sports leaders and the athlete with the greatest number of votes (three for first, two for second, etc.) receives the trophy.

Usually an athlete is nominated at least once or twice before the honor comes his way. Gil, however, won it the first time his name was submitted! He received a total of 860 votes, almost twice as many as the second place winner, Bill Smith, a swimmer from

Ohio State university. Joe Platak, a handball player from Chicago, was third with 425.

When the official notice reached his home Gil told a reporter of a Boston paper, "I've often dreamed about getting it, but felt that it was too much of a dream. Now I feel that God made it possible."

Writers and athletic heads lauded the selection. The summer before they had written that if Gil Dodds had had an ounce of conceit in him, he would have licked Hagg in their races. The adjectives rolled out: "Modest, unassuming, honest, cleancut, pure .... the kind of an athlete who some day will be able to stand up in a pulpit and look his congregation square in the eye."

Newspapermen wrote such words as the following:

"He exemplifies all of the characteristics of a perfect gentleman and sportsman. Modest in victory and gracious in defeat. By precept and example he is a splendid influence on all with whom he comes in contact. Has always been willing to cooperate with any organization conducting track meets when such requests tend to help and promote interest in his favorite sport. Exemplified by his willingness to race anywhere against anyone from one to three miles."

* * *

"There's not a small bone in his body. He does his training at a Jesuit college under a coach who is a devout Catholic. He tries to set an example and, perhaps, to lead men to better things. But he never intrudes. He doesn't put the squeeze on the promoters for expense money they would willingly give. He would not think of padding his expense account."

* * *

"An unquenchable typification of the ideal amateur athlete."

* * *

"Dodds never failed to do his best."

* * *

From Greg Rice: "Gil is a great runner and has a great heart. He is one of the best there is along any line."

* * *

"Never given to an athlete who more typified its meaning."

* * *

He is so sincere in his idealism that many of his fellow contemporaries think that he is a chump, but a chump who must be admired and respected."

* * *

"He knows that this isn't a world of innocence and purity, and he knows, in his way, how to make it a better world. Yet he never points a finger at his fellow humans, whether in the sports world or outside."

* * *

"Unspoiled by fame . . . modest as a choir boy . . . American as apple pie . . . the kind of a fellow you'd like to have for a son or brother."

* * *

"As becoming a figure in athletics as we've ever had. The purest athlete of modern times."

* * *

"Stout fella, and a real champion." (John Kieran, New York Times, at that time).

* * *

These words and many more rambled off the pens of writers and sport luminaries. The selection of Gil Dodds as the winner of the 1943 Sullivan trophy was greeted with acclaim from sport fans everywhere. L. di Benedetto, president of the Amateur Athletic union, gave this statement,

"I don't know of a finer sportsman than Gil Dodds. His willingness to tour America last year with Gunder Hagg was a splendid gesture; he did it because he was a sportsman, knowing full well that he could hardly expect to beat this wonderful Swedish athlete. He is a splendid athlete, sportsman, and Christian, and it was a pleasure for me to present him with this award."

* * *

Grantland Rice, dean of American sportswriters, wrote,

"He is a fine combination of a great athlete and a great sportsman. He also happens to be one of the greatest competitors we have had in a long time."

And how did Gil Dodds feel about all this? What did he think about the praise of the sports writers who remember him best for his graciousness in defeat, not his happiness in triumph, a man who unfailingly gives credit to his conqueror?

Gil said his piece to thousands of fans gathered on February 26, 1944, in New York when he was presented the award. The champ declared,

"This is the high spot in my life, the winning of this award. I know, and I want the world to know, that only through God have I been able to achieve the athletic prowess I've enjoyed. I want to pass on to younger athletes a bit of advice. I urge them always to live up to the high ideals exemplified by the A. A. U. and to strive for the higher and spiritual life which all must live if they expect success in any kind of endeavor."

The Sullivan award was his, and it fitted him well because once more he proved his worth by giving all credit for it to God. It's hard to take defeat, even at the hands of a truly great champion such as Gunder Hagg, but once more Gil Dodds proved the truth of the Bible passage found in Luke 13:30, "And behold, there are last which shall be first, and there are first which shall be last."

* * *

Winter of 1944 was here in Boston, just as in every other part of the United States. Cross country and indoor drills since September 1, 1943, had keyed Gil to a training pitch Jack Ryder hoped he would reach. The Sullivan award also helped Gil; it gave him added confidence. Through December and January Ryder and Dodds worked endlessly and tirelessly to get the "Flying Parson" into shape. This was to be "his" year, or the start of a series of years when he hoped to reach the peak and stay there.

As usual, the Millrose games opened the indoor season on the first Saturday in February. Gil was among the entrants but for once something other than track was occupying his mind. In Boston his wife was expecting a baby and so anxious was Gil about the arrival of the offspring that he missed his usual train to New York. For a while track officials wondered if he would get to New York in time, but he made it. "With the stork wings flapping in unison," Gil won the Millrose mile race in 4:10.6 minutes, not a record time but still fast enough for the opener.

But it wasn't until the following Thursday that little John Lloyd Dodds, named after Jack Ryder and Lloyd Hahn, put in his appearance. Gil explained the naming of "Jackie," as he is called, this way:

"We had agreed that if it was a girl Erma could name her. If a boy, I could. Well, you know how women are. After Jackie was born she thought it would be nice to name him John Lloyd, and so did I, so we did."

Two days after Jackie arrived Gil raced in the Boston A.A. games in the Boston Garden and nudged his time down to 4:09.5 minutes, "just for Jackie." A week later in New York it was whittled down to 4:08 minutes. In an exhibition race the next week it slipped back to 4:10.2 minutes. But on March 11, 1944, Gil Dodds opened another door to the track's hall of fame by clipping one-tenth of a second from the world's indoor mile record, winning the Knights of Columbus race in the Garden in 4:07.3 minutes. The old record of 4:07.4 minutes was held jointly by Glenn Cunningham, Charles Fenske and Les MacMitchell.

A few minutes later he amazed the packed Garden crowd by roaring back to win the 1,000 meter race, thus completing the first double triumph in the Garden since 1935 when the peerless Cunningham did it.

But he wasn't through yet.

A year previous he had won the Banker's Mile in the Chicago Daily News Relays, the same event which Lloyd Hahn had won three years in succession when he was in his prime. Now, seven days after setting the mark in New York, he stepped onto the Chicago Stadium track again and broke the world record for the indoor mile by 9/10 of a second, slicing it down 4:06.4 minutes. A few hours after setting that record he was on his way to Goshen, Ind., to preach a sermon the next day before returning to Boston and seminary classes.

Even headlines in newspapers give credit to the Lord when a story on Gil Dodds is written. After his record attempt in New York a headline read,

"WHEN I RAN I PRAYED — DODDS"

* * *

When he ran in Chicago the headline read,
"THE LORD, HAHN, GIL
    COLLABORATE ON MARK"
Even that headline writer knew Gil's Christian philosophy of "the Lord first, others next and myself last."

The final race of the 1944 indoor season found Gil reverting back to his favorite two-mile in a meet at Cleveland, Ohio. A bad ankle turn kept him from setting a record although he did win the race to end the season without a defeat and take rank with Glenn Cunningham and Charles Fenske as the only athletes who have won all of the races in a single season.

Spring came, and then summer. The Red Cross asked Gil to run in an exhibition in New York but once again the Gospel call came first as he felt bound to keep an appointment to preach in his father's church at Smithville, Ohio. He had hoped, too, to defend his Northeast A.A.U. championship on June 9 and his national A.A.U. title on June 17, but plans had been made for a 16-state speaking tour of army camps, naval bases, youth conferences, etc., and so those two titles went undefended.

From Sweden came an invitation to come over and run against Gunder Hagg and Arne Andersson, Hagg's great competitor there. Once more the temptation was great; Gil never has been abroad and the desire to run was strong. However, the desire to serve the Lord was stronger and the invitation was declined with sincere regrets.

Gil hasn't been sorry that he followed that course during the summer of 1944. All along the way the Lord proved to him by the response to his talks and messages that his testimony of the saving power of the Lord Jesus Christ was winning people to Christ. He spoke 158 times in three and a half months, spanning

16 states and addressing at least 50,000 people directly and countless thousands of others through the radio and press. In meetings at three army camps in the South—Fort Bragg, N. C., Fort Jackson, S. C., and Camp Gordon, Ga.—he held 28 services with the Pocket Testament league team of Glenn Warner, former Illinois football star, and himself. At those camps he spoke to 20,000 men and 2,100 of them made a profession of Christ as their personal Saviour.

Traveling with Jack Wyrtzen, director of New York's "Word of Life" hour, he saw 400 young people accept the Lord. In Montana, with the Christ for America movement led by Horace Dean, he spread-eagled the state in two and a half weeks of meetings, reaching approximately 40 per cent of the people in the state either in meetings or over the radio. Here, too, many souls were won for the Lord.

To Winona Lake, Ind., for its world-famous Bible conference, to Moody Bible Institute's Labor Day rally, to "Youth for Christ" meetings at St. Louis, Indianapolis, Chicago, New York and other cities throughout the land, to Chicago and 16 meetings in four days with dynamic Torrey Johnson, Gil moved with his testimony of what the Lord had done for him on the track. Thousands of Bibles and New Testaments today carry the famous Gil Dodds autograph with a Bible verse as a result of the summer's traveling. Countless numbers of Christian young people were strengthened in their own lives by his testimony.

Gil had left Boston on June 2, the day after his spring examinations were over. He returned to Boston and his final semester at Gordon School of Theology and Missions on the day that students were registering for the term. His summer hadn't been spent in chasing

Gunder Hagg around a track but he was still his athletic and in-condition self. It had been a busy summer and a hard summer, but Gil Dodds had given out freely that which the Lord had given him.

Classes were started and in that position we leave Gil Dodds, as far as the year by year story of his life is concerned. Safely back in their Boston apartment are the three members of the Dodds family—Gil, Erma and Jackie. The future looks promising to this fine little trio; God has first place in their hearts and lives and they all know that whether defeats or victories are on the slate of the future that "All things work together for good to them that love God and are the called according to His purpose."

What Gil Dodds will do when he is graduated from Gordon School of Theology and Missions in 1945 no one except the Lord knows. He might be in the service as a chaplain, he might be headed for some foreign mission field, he might be working in a youth organization, he might be serving a small country church in rural New England.

But wherever he goes he says, and sings,

"If Jesus goes with me, I'll go, anywhere."

Chapter VII

LITTLE BIT OF EVERYTHING

In writing this story of Gil Dodds we have chosen to leave a goodly number of sidelights and human interest stories about Gil until this chapter. Each could have been fitted into a proper place and position in the past chapters, as you've read in greater and less detail the story of how Gil reached the top.

Even though we open ourselves to criticism on repetition of something previously said, we must say once more that Gil is decidedly human. He enjoys the same little things, such as fried chicken, as you do. He doesn't feel superior at all because fame has been his; it has come his way, he feels, because God gave him the ability to let it be his if he used it to the glory of God. Every time you talk to him he seems to emphasize that it doesn't take the best to reach the top; hard work and a definite dependence on the Lord are two fundamental requirements.

* * *

Perhaps the thing for which he is known the most among non-Christians is the way in which he signs his autograph. *Every time* he signs it, whether it be a minute or two after a hard two-mile race or following a Gospel appeal in a church or any place else, the "Gil Dodds" will be followed by a verse of Scripture.

It's not always the same verse, nor always his favorite verse. His favorite passage in the Bible happens to be Hebrews 12:1-2,

"Wherefore seeing we also are compassed

about with so great a cloud of witnesses, let us lay aside every weight, and the sin which doth so easily beset us, and let us run with patience the race that is set before us,

"Looking unto Jesus the author and finisher of our faith; who for the joy that was set before Him endured the cross, despising the shame, and is set down on the right hand of the throne of God."

Often he adds his "life" verse, found in Philippians 4:13,

"I can do all things through Christ, which strengtheneth me."

Or it might be Isaiah 40:31, the verse that meant so much to him when he was trying to decide for or against the Lord:

"But they that wait upon the Lord shall renew their strength; they shall mount up with wings as eagles; they shall run, and not be weary; and they shall walk, and not faint."

Whatever the verse might be, there is a message in it. Gil has found 60 passages in the Bible which refer to athletics, and as the Lord gives him opportunity to use them with his autograph he does so.

When you think of the number of times which he signs his name during a year and compare it with the chances which he gets to follow up his testimony by talking to the person about salvation you get a small percentage. The necessary time isn't there after races or after big meetings. Gil has felt, however, that God's Word will not return unto Him void and so he continues to add the Scripture verse and ask God to use it to lead someone to the cross.

He has signed his autograph thousands upon thousands of times. A girl in Chicago asked him, after hav-

— 65 —

ing him sign a scorecard, "Is that your phone number?" A lady in New York wrote to him that she and her daughter had sat up until 4 a.m. after getting Gil's autograph, checking and following up the Scripture passages which his verse had led to.

Every time he signs an entry blank he adds a Bible verse. Track meet promoters need the Gospel, too, he reasoned, and in one meet he signed the blank, "Gil Dodds, Hebrews 12:1-2."

The promoter decided to look it up. As he read the first part he was glad . . . *"Wherefore seeing we also are compassed about with so great a cloud of witnesses . . . . ."* This meant a great crowd, and promoters like great crowds.

But he read on, *". . . . . . let us lay aside every weight and the sin that doth so easily beset us, and let us run with patience the race that is set before us."*

He checked that last part. "Run with patience." That didn't fit so well when he was expecting a world's record; he knew that runners didn't set world's records running *patiently!*

But no promoter ever has had to worry about Gil Dodds running a foot race with patience; it just isn't in him. He is out to win from the beginning and runs accordingly.

Gil always carries a Bible in his pocket in case anyone wants to check the verse on the spot. So widespread has his autograph become known that one writer referred to it as "A sermon with every signature." Gil's own reaction, as stated above, is to implant the Word of God in the heart of each person who receives his autograph. He told one reporter, "If through my autograph I can inspire a single soul to return to the path of the Lord I will have achieved a greater victory than the breaking of any track record."

A few minutes after his record performance in Chicago Gil was getting a rubdown in the locker room. The pliable fingers of the expert soothed the tired muscles that had just moved Gil to a new world record. Gil was resting, his eyes shut. He opened them after a few minutes, caught the eye of a man standing by the door, and nodded. The man slipped out of the door and in a moment was back with ten youngsters in tow.

One by one they handed their New Testaments to Gil. One by one he signed his name and a Bible verse and added a word of encouragement. They looked at their Testaments, then at Gil, then quietly moved out of the locker room. The next week most likely found ten proud boys on playgrounds in Chicago showing their playmates the autograph of the champion and explaining what the Bible verse meant. And so the Word is spread.

A story in "Yank," the service newspaper, by Sgt. Dan Polier, written in a semi-humorous vein, attributes the sale of two million more Bibles in 1943 to "Deacon Dodds." Polier writes,

"Gil Dodds has done more for the American Bible Society than anyone since King James. He signs his name and the autograph seekers dash for the nearest book store and buy a Bible." Polier adds that in such manner Gil has been known to sell more than 15,000 Bibles in a single night.

Polier explains a typical scene after a big race. He suggests that reporters now come with Bibles in order to better check the passages to which Gil likely will refer. After breaking the record in the New York race Gil faced his "congregation" of reporters and said,

"The good Lord was with me tonight. I never doubted he would give me the necessary strength if only I didn't quit on myself. Yes, I prayed while I ran."

Along with his autograph Gil now is using Gospel tracts, feeling that by that means he can better follow up on people who might not know what the verse after his name means.

The autograph has brought him many chances to open the way of salvation to people who later write him. Often, after winning a race, he will sign his name and add the verse. A day later when he gets home he will find a letter asking for a little more information and help in such and such a verse. Many of the people who write in are youngsters, including athletes, and through this letter-writing Gil has the chance to reach them for Christ.

An old man in New York looked at the autograph he received on his scorecard and said,

"H-m-m. Phil. 4:13. That '4:13' must be his best time of four minutes and thirteen seconds, and that 'Phil.' must mean that he made it in Philadelphia."

As one reporter wrote, Gil doesn't intrude. He doesn't make himself a pest by constantly talking "religion." Rather, he waits for opportunities to witness, and then uses them.

A train was late in leaving Winona Lake, Ind., where Gil had spoken at that internationally-known Bible conference grounds. Gil slipped into town for a bite to eat, he and a friend each taking a seat alongside a little boy at a counter. First thing you knew Gil was talking to the little fellow.

"You go to Sunday School, pal?"

"Naw, I don't go."

Before Gil was through talking to him he had promised to attend the next day. Into the little boy's pocket went a tract with Gil's picture on it and the famous autograph under it. Even as they walked out of the restaurant there was time to slip a tract into the hand of the fellow in high school behind the counter who recognized Gil as soon as he came in.

With the autograph comes the handshake. Not the pulverizing kind, but the firm, solid handshake of a man who knows his purpose in life. Gil has shaken hands with more people than perhaps he would care to remember. For each of them he has the ever-ready smile and the humble "Well, thanks, but the Lord did it for me."

Gil laughs every time he thinks of one hand-shaking experience after a race. After it was over Gil found it extremely hard to reach the car in which he was supposed to go to the station as the crowd of admirers hemmed him in. Finally he slipped into a nearby car, circled the block and came back. When he hopped out of that car into the one he was going to the station in, a little fellow with tattered clothes spied him and ran up, saying, "Can I shake your hand, Mr. Dodds?"

Gil shook his hand, and just as he was getting into the car this little fellow smiled and said,

"Boy, that's the fourth time tonight."

Through all of the crowds, and all of the autographs Gil has remained the perfect gentleman. Sometimes crowds aren't too easy on him but unless he has to catch a train he will stay and give his signature to anyone that wants it. He's humble and wise enough to realize that there isn't much value in his name and that in a few years it well might fade away.

He remembers, however, that the Scripture verse underneath never will pass away.

GIL AND HIS FAMILY

No higher tribute could be given to Erma Louise Seeger Dodds, Gil's extremely pleasant and capable wife, than Gil paid her when asked which person had had the most influence on his Christian life.

He answered briefly and surely,

"My wife."

Gil met Erma Louise Seeger, daughter of fine Christian parents, soon after Gil's father moved to Falls City to assume the pastoral work there. He was a junior in high school and she was a sophomore. As soon as they started keeping company they realized that as far as they were concerned they would have to look no more at anyone of the opposite sex. The young fellow with the heavy mop of hair that liked to stick up as though freshly washed was solidly in love with the girl with the pleasant smile and the air of being in control of every situation.

When Gil's dad moved to Mexico, Ind. the summer after Gil finished high school Gil easily found two jobs in Falls City to keep him busy . . . and near Erma. He worked in a bakery and a library and when he wasn't working he was either training or seeing Erma.

That was in the summer of 1937. A few months later, on the last day of the year — a few hours before the dawn of 1938 — Gil and Erma were married in Indianapolis, Indiana.

Their one son, Jackie, is a regular little boy, rough and tough as they come, although not yet a year old at this writing. Gil likes to pick him up by one foot and one arm in taking him out of a car and wants to make a man out of him in a hurry. The three of them form one of the happiest Christian families which God ever has placed together. They live in a modest apartment in

Boston, not far from the Gordon College of Theology and Missions, where Gil attends.

Jackie arrived on February 9, 1944, and since that time Gil has yet to lose a race. Even during the added work which Jackie's coming meant — as cooking for himself, keeping things in the apartment clean, etc. — Gil managed to stay in tip-top shape and keep on winning races.

Mrs. Dodds is a fine cook and to her goes much of the credit for keeping the "Perambulating Parson" in shape. Jack Ryder calls her "Gil's second coach," and she does take up where Ryder leaves off in keeping an eagle eye on the habits of her famous husband. Gil sums it up tersely, "Everything Erma cooks is body-building, so why should I kick?"

Gil has the athlete's appetite — good and large. One of his favorite dishes when in training is a "good pound steak." These come often when Gil is in training, ration points willing. One time Gil came home from a week-end and had gotten in with a bunch of vegetarians. Ryder noticed something wrong right away in Monday's drill and slowly pulled the story out of him. Training was over for that day and Gil went home to exist on a meat diet for almost 24 hours. Then he was his normal self.

He dotes on bread. When working at the hotel during college days the student newspaper once carried these words, "Men mowed down by machine guns could fall no more quickly nor in larger numbers than the slices of bread which daily tumble into the Dodds bread basket."

* * *

During the track season Gil doesn't read the sports pages of newspapers. Mrs. Dodds takes a scissors and snips out the sports pages before he comes home from training. They have two reasons for doing this. First is that if Gil spends too much time on the newspapers he won't have enough time for studying. The second is the feeling that most of the stories are just so much propaganda, with plenty of advice on how Gil can reach the four-minute mile "if he just does this, etc." A friend on a Boston newspaper, George Carens of the Boston HERALD, snips out stories for Gil during the season and gives them to him when the season is over. In this way Gil feels that he will not be swayed by what sportswriters might think of his running, pacing, etc.

On the way home from New York after breaking the world record on March 11, 1944, Gil pulled out a sandwich and apple and shared them with Ryder. So thorough is Mrs. Dodds about seeing that Gil stays in tiptop shape that she even had the trip home planned on that race.

Usually after a race Gil will drink up to two quarts of milk in his hotel room. Sometimes he'll add a honey sandwich. His sense of humor keeps cropping out at the most unusual times. Once as he and Mrs. Dodds were about to leave New York for Boston and the reporters were still standing around, eager to use any word Gil might say in their stories, he remarked to his wife,

"Honey, let's stop for a bottle . . . " and as the reporters looked at each other in surprise, he added, . . . "of milk on the way home."

He likes apples, oranges, nuts, raisins and honey. Often when he walks to and from training at Boston College he will have a carrot in his pocket on which he will nibble. He's a good bread-maker as well as breadwinner and often has done the family washing to help his wife along.

Mrs. Dodds was along on part of the trip in 1943 when Gil raced Hagg. It was sort of a second honeymoon for them and they tried to make the most of it.

* * *

Before every race Gil can feel her prayers for him. He told reporters in Chicago on that record-breaking night that "Knowing that my wife is with me in her prayers, asking that the Lord's will might be done even in this race, helps an awful lot. She's a real moral asset, too. Her fine Christian parents also have helped me a good deal in my running through their encouragement and especially in that it can be used as a testimony for Christ."

Because of Gil's frequent trips Mrs. Dodds has had to be home alone quite a bit. She realizes, however, that the Lord's work comes first and both Gil and she have agreed that Gil's running is the main way in which he can lead men and women to Christ at this time.

Some day, if the Lord tarries and leads Gil to a church, she'll make an ideal pastor's wife. She is as sweet, kind, considerate, and fine as wives and mothers come and the type of a help which even such a famous man as Gil Dodds needs, appreciates and thanks God for.

* * *

GIL DODDS — ATHLETE

To most Americans Gil Dodds is known as an athlete. To them he is "The Champ," and as such a few words on his track achievements and abilities are in order.

He's not a big man. He weighs 148 pounds when in

condition and stands five feet nine inches. He doesn't look like an athlete the first time you see him and your first reaction is that he's much smaller than you had expected. Few people recognize him on the street, or did until the last year or so, for which he is thankful.

He has a powerful set of legs, a wonderful body and a strong heart. Ever since he started to run, people have told him that he never could be a great miler because he lacked a sprint, or final kick. But in that Gil has fooled them all. He might not have the sprint, but he does have *stamina*. And stamina has been winning race after race for Gil Dodds.

Track experts, in analyzing the possibility of the four-minute mile, contend that a runner to do that must be able to run a quarter of a mile in 48 seconds. Gil cannot go that fast — his best time for a quarter of a mile is 52 and 53 seconds. But where he lacks in speed, he makes up for in stamina and power. For that he gives credit to the Lord. "Instead of speed which most athletes have," he explained, "the Lord gave me an extra dose of stamina and staying power."

This is how Gil will run a race:

As soon as the gun goes off he starts at one steady pace. Usually in the opening yards he will lose a second or two in finding his place on the track, especially if the field is large. At the end of the first lap he generally is behind. In the second and third laps he moves ahead and usually takes the lead as the other runners save themselves a bit for the final stretch drive. In recent years the lead which he builds up in the second and third quarters has been sufficient to withstand any sprint by his opponents.

However, in Gil's record-breaking nights at New York and Chicago he did have a "kick" left. With only the crowd to spur him on at Chicago he unloosed the strong finish which put him nine-tenths of a second under the record. In 100-yard dashes he cannot better 11.3 seconds, whereas other distance runners get down as low as 10 seconds.

Hagg and Gil stopped at Harvard university's fatigue laboratory when on their tour. The charts on Gil's tests astounded the scientists! They found that in running Gil develops enough acid to kill the average human being! In the matter of getting back to normal coordination after a race, Gil's test showed 120. The average is 60 to 65! That explains why two minutes after a gruelling race Gil is almost his normal self.

Gil produces sugar as he runs and as it is manufactured by his body he gets added stamina. This is the key to his great ability to run, run, run and run some more without stopping.

However, a physique and ability do not make a champion. The training grind must be gone through. Gil has trained thousands of hours in getting in shape for races. He once told a reporter, "I train as though everything depends on me and pray as though everything depends on God."

Take a look at his training schedule and you'll see how much work he actually does.

On or around Labor Day of every year he starts his cross country work. In this he will run and walk anywhere from five to ten miles a day. This continues until around December 1, with perhaps a couple of cross country meets thrown in on the way, when he starts his indoor drills on the board tracks. This keeps up until the first week in February, when he finally is set for a race, and on through the indoor season.

That adds up to five months of training before he is ready for a **single race!**

A regular day in Boston finds him reaching the Boston College track at three o'clock after a five-mile walk from Gordon College. In the off-season he will work on sprints for a half hour, with four to six practice starts after a warmup of 10 or 15 minutes. Then he slowly jogs a mile and takes his exercises before he reports to Ryder for his workout of the day. About 4 or 4:30 p. m. he is through. After a shower he will walk five miles home some days and take a streetcar on others to be ready for a heavy supper. In the evening, after studying for a few hours, he will walk two or three miles before retiring between 9:30 and 10 p. m.

When he returns from a meet and has spent extra time on the train he will walk an extra five or seven miles. The day he arrived home from Chicago with the world's record in his pocket he found Boston in a blizzard. The train was late and in order to make up for that extra time of sitting down he walked three more miles through wind and snow.

Walking to him is one of the best conditioners there is and he follows Ryder's orders explicitly along that line. Gil is the greatest trainer that Ryder ever has coached; he won't spare himself in practice in order to get into shape. Ryder once said of him,

"He is a modern Spartan, perfectly willing to subject himself to the most exacting regimen."

Gil's marvelous pacing ability has been touched upon but it bears repetition. It has been said that he adjusts himself like a metronome. He is never more than a second or two off when Ryder orders him to run a distance in a certain time. He is to running what Bobby Jones was to golf: both play against par and forget their opponents. Ryder and Gil get together before a race and map out the time Gil should take for each lap and each quarter. Often his opponents try to upset that plan by running faster in the first quarter, or slowing him down, but he usually makes up for it on the next lap.

Track experts hardly rave about his "style" of running. He isn't a beautiful picture of grace as he runs but the manner in which he puts one foot down after the other is a pleasure to watch. He has a very long stride and runs with an arm-flailing, head-rolling style. But, the experts add in the next breath, "How he can pour it on!"

Most distance runners "train up" to the mile, that is, by starting with the shorter distances and then reaching the mile. Gil has been just the opposite. He is a long distance runner who has trained down.

He runs with his glasses on. His eyes aren't bad but he is far-sighted and has a little astigmatism. Also, he is slightly color blind when it comes to distinguishing between green and red.

One thing which few people know about Gil is that he has a hernia. He never has used it as an alibi for any defeat. In every race he wears a truss to protect himself. In this respect he is like Greg Rice, who has a double hernia. It developed in his junior year in high school when he was playing tennis and reached too fast for a high ball.

When he walks he seems to have a little spring in his step. Since his sophomore year in college he has averaged 10,000 miles per season in going to meets, etc. Someone wondered out loud once how many thousands of miles he ever has run or walked in practice or in meets. Gil didn't even want to estimate it.

Someone asked Gil about getting conceited about his feats and Gil replied this way,

"The Lord gave me my talent of running so there's no reason for me to get conceited about it. The defeats have come and I know they have been for my own good. In each one the Lord has taught me something definite."

As great as Dodds is physically, he is still greater spiritually. Which is why we look at another side of him.

* * *

"I PRAY ABOUT MY RUNNING"

A headline in the New York paper read,

"I prayed as I ran — Dodds."

It's true.

Being a real Christian, Gil pray's about everything he does. As stated in the opening chapter, he prays a good deal before a race. He doesn't pray alone, either, because all over the country he has picked up "prayer warriors" who remember him as he races.

Lewis Burton, a sports writer on the New York *Journal American*, once asked Gil what prayer he prayed so he could pass it on to aspiring athletes. Gil answered, "You don't need any special prayers from the Bible to address the Lord. You speak from the heart and He will understand."

Often people will stop him after a defeat and say,

"What happened, Dodds? Didn't the Lord hear your prayers?"

And Gil replies,

"I didn't pray the Lord that He would let me win. I just asked Him to give me the strength to do my best and for added strength after all of mine is used up."

Gil neglected to pray before one race and the Lord

taught him a lesson through it. He won the race handily but for two days after he was almost exhausted. He knows the reason now — no prayer and an entire dependence on himself and not God.

After the record breaking race in New York a merchant marine man walked up to Gil and asked him for an interview. Gil said "Sure" so up to his hotel room they went. After Gil had answered his questions and the fellow was about to go, he asked,

"Do you believe in prayer?"

"I sure do," Gil answered. "Why?"

"Well," the merchant mariner said, "before I came down here tonight two of my buddies and myself had a prayer meeting and asked the Lord to allow you to set a world's record tonight. And He answered!"

Gil believes in consistent and daily prayer, not only before a race or test. However, in that fleeting moment before the gun goes off to start a race he utters a quick prayer to God for help during the race.

Letters from boys warm Gil's heart. Just before a big race he received a letter from a little fellow which read, "I won't be able to see you run, but I'll be praying that you will win and set a record. I asked God to let you run the mile in 3:57 minutes tonight."

Some people might say, "Well, why not the four-minute mile if God is helping you along so much?"

Gil's reply to that has been, "The Lord will help us in anything we do if it's to His glory that it be done. But we must remember that prayer isn't the only thing. It's an important and necessary part in anything we do, but we must do our part."

Christians have a comforting slogan which reads, "Prayer changes things." In Gil's case that has been changed to "Prayer changes records."

* * *
GLIMPSES HERE AND THERE
Few people know that when Gil ran in his first big-time race in the Sugar Bowl on New Year's Day, 1939, he ran in a track suit which his wife had remodeled from a suit of underwear. Few people know, too, that he likes to buy a new pair of shoe strings for every race . . . and that he doesn't like to have his wife wash any track pants in which he has started a winning streak and in which he never has been defeated.

* * *

Gil always has been able to get along with newspapermen. They have placed many funny things after his name, as "Epistle Packing Pastor," "Flying Parson," "Perambulating Parson," etc., but Gil hasn't minded it a bit. One reporter wrote, "He wouldn't run on Sunday, not even for a streetcar." Gil takes every chance he can get to speak about the Lord, even to reporters. Most of the reporters are not Christians but they have been decent and fair to Gil. Especially to Bill McKee and to writers in Boston, as Jerry Nason, George Carens and others does Gil extend a real thank you for the help which they have given him.

* * *

As a youngster Gil was interested in scouting and also served as an assistant scoutmaster for a period. He achieved the rank of Eagle scout (gold palm) as he moved ahead rapidly once started.

* * *

He doesn't sing much, nor does he play any musical instruments. . . His favorite subject in school is theology, with archaeology second. . .Sometimes after running in a smoke-filled arena he will have a sore throat for a week because of the smoke. . . His constant aim is to talk to every runner against whom he competes about the Lord Jesus Christ.

* * *

Up until a few years ago he often went to a movie just before he raced. He hoped it would relax his mind and take his thoughts from the race but he usually found that it was the other way around. When he toured the country with Hagg and had an opportunity to visit Hollywood he was more convinced than ever that he never would patronize movies again.

While on the way out to one of the studios in Hollywood Gil started to talk to the chauffeur. The man remarked to him,

"Say, I can't figure you Christians out at all. That's why I'm an atheist."

Then he told his story. A certain picture, religious in nature, had been filmed, and had not the churches endorsed it, it would have been a complete financial flop. But that wasn't the rub. He went on to explain that it was his duty every night to see to it that all of the actors and actresses were safely home after the day's work. Day after day he had to take drunken show people home late at night after they had worked on a "religious" picture all day.

And, he added, the man who played the part of Jesus Christ in the picture was the worst of them all.

That trip "cured" Gil of Hollywood and motion pictures as produced there. His fiery testimony, too, has been directed against what he regards as an evil and not a benefit as far as recreation and amusement for young people is concerned. As for himself, Gil is one of the multitude of candid camera fans and usually takes his motion picture camera along with him on every trip.

* * *

His various jobs going through school have found him employed as a life guard, in a bakery, in orchards, running a trap line, various odd jobs, in a hotel and on a highway crew... When idle he packs on weight fairly fast... His traveling has given him poise, but not hypocrisy.

* * *

One day while working along a road in Mexico, Ind., where his father was pastor, he heard the cry of a drowning boy. An expert swimmer, he was at the river in a moment. He ripped his clothes off and on the third dive reached the 15-year-old lad. He dragged him to the shore and started artificial respiration. For two hours he worked over him, but failed to revive him.

* * *

Several incidents stand out in Gil's life as far as any influence he might have had on other people. One such instance took place on the record-setting night in New York. As Gil was getting dressed in the locker room a young fellow approached him and asked Gil if he would wear something in the race. Gil asked him what it was, and the fellow showed him a crucifix.

Gil said that he didn't believe he needed the crucifix to win, but he insisted. Gil stalled him off by agreeing to meet him in the locker room after the first race and that he would wear it in the second race — the 1,000 yard event.

Between races Gil waited and waited but the lad didn't show up. Gil half expected to see him out near the track, but still there was no sight of him during the warmups. Just as the contestants were ready to go to the line and the infield had been cleared, the fellow broke past a guard, ran down to Gil, handed him the crucifix and then bolted back to the sidelines. Gil didn't know what to do, so he slipped it into a fold in his track pants and wore it during the race. He won that race, too, though he was sure it wasn't because of the crucifix.

Later Gil contacted the fellow and they became real friends. Gil was able to sit down with him and show him the way of salvation through the blood of Jesus Christ. He accepted the Lord as his personal Saviour at a Saturday night "Word of Life" rally in Madison Square Garden, and after correspondence with Gil seems ready to go into full-time Christian service as a medical doctor.

* * *

In the summer of 1944 Gil spoke at a youth meeting. In the afternoon he had given an exhibition at the local Y.M.C.A. and a boy there had seen him and admired him, as he too was a trackman. Gil invited him to the evening service and he came and sat through it all. After it was over Gil noticed him lingering, waiting until the autograph-seekers had left. The first thing the fellow said was, "You know, I want to be saved, but I just don't know how to go about it." Gil knew . . . and the Bible that never leaves him was put into use once more to lead a soul to Christ.

* * *

More than a score of national magazines have had articles on Gil, including Liberty, Scholastic, American, Magazine Digest, Life, Time, worldly-toned Esquire, Newsweek, and others in the secular field, and Sunday, Christian Herald, Watchman-Examiner, Protestant Voice, The Evangelical Beacon, and many others in the religious field.

* * *

There was a time when he hesitated to ask for a free ticket to a meet for his wife. Another time he lost his contestant's ticket and rather than explain his way through the gate he paid the tax on a complimentary ticket which he had... When Gil wins a race the mail goes way up; when he loses it sags.

* * *

Gil is said to have set an all-time speed record when working at the Hotel Otter in Ashland and the hotel clerk gave a customer $5 too much in change when he paid his bill. They gave Gil the "go sign" and he caught the man at the depot just before he got on the train.

* * *

A glimpse into a Rotary club meeting and the voice of Gil Dodds is heard saying, "Life must be Christ-centered if it is to mean anything." .. A glimpse into a letter from the South Pacific tells of a lieutenant colonel writing to ask Gil for copies of a certain speech which Gil had made. Said the officer, "We want that type of talk. It's what we need for our boys."

* * *

A glimpse into the Dodds apartment finds a beautiful 63-piece silver set which Gil and his wife received from a Swedish group in Boston for racing against Gunder Hagg... A look at a day of practicing might bring into view one of Gil's hero worshippers, a boy from Newton, Mass., who goes through *exactly* the same warmup and workout which Gil does even though he is training to be a pole vaulter.

* * *

A glance at the comparative records of Glenn Cunningham, known to the world as "Mr. Mile" and one of Gil's heroes, gives Gil the upper hand. Whereas Cunningham ran only five races under 4:09 minutes in five years, Gil ran nine under 4:09 in three years. Cunningham perhaps never had anyone who idolized him as much as Gil did when he was growing up. The great Kansan, who was told by doctors when only eight years old that he never would walk again, always has stood high in Gil's memory.

* * *

A careful *look* at the side of Gil's neck might reveal a small scar. Until the summer of 1944 he had a small growth there which hardened and became annoying after each race. An operation that summer took care of that.

* * *

A *check* through his souvenirs finds a tattered contestant's number with these words on the back: "To a friend with highest regards. Cornelius Warmerdam." A strong and mutual friendship has developed between Gil and the great pole vaulter. It's a spiritual friendship, too, because Warmerdam stops to pray before every jump he attempts.

* * *

Seeing the humorous side of Dodds is easy to do as he has so much of it. One example: "I only hope I don't lower the records so low that my son can't break them." . . A lady in New York wrote Gil that she had had a revelation that Gil was one of the 12 disciples and that he should stop at a certain address in New York on his next trip and meet the other eleven.

Gil didn't stop.

* * *

He always has met people who insist that it's impossible to be a Christian and an athlete at the same time. One old man backed it up with Scripture when he quoted Psalm 147:10, ". . . He taketh not pleasure in the legs of a man." In another church, one in which Gil had spent some of his early years, a man refused to come to church when he heard that Gil was going to preach. "Athletics are sinful," he said.

* * *

One fan mail letter disturbed him for a while. It came from one Sydney Dodds of New Orleans and traced Gil's lineage in the Dodds family tree back through a Pennsylvania branch and thence to the Mayflower, winding up with a blast at Gil for being the first Dodds in history who has failed to bear arms in defense of his country. As far as the service goes, Gil has been advised by the head of chaplains of the First Corps Area to finish his seminary work first and then apply.

* * *

Gil once ran against a horse!

It happened at the Ashland county fair in Ashland, Ohio. As a special feature of the fair Gil had three races with a horse named Peter at Law. He ran a half mile and the horse a mile. (One lady wrote to the newspaper and said that the race was unfair because the horse had someone on his back urging him along and Gil didn't have anyone!)

The horse won the first race, and collected a package of oats. Gil won the second . . . and a pair of pants. In the final "rubber" race, Gil won . . . and with it a suitcase.

* * *

Horses or men, Gil has given his best every time he has raced. He's an ideal Christian, happy in the place in which the Lord has placed him and giving all glory and credit to God for any honors which have come his way. To the Christian world that modest, unassuming and God-glorifying nature is one to be sought after; to the world it is at times hard to explain.

But because of it people tend to turn around and say, "I wish I had what he has."

Chapter VIII

WITNESSING WITH HIS LIPS

BECAUSE of his high position in the sports world Gil Dodds has had many opportunities presented to him to speak. In many of those cases the people listening to him perhaps would be satisfied with a good moral talk on living a clean life in order to be a successful athlete. But Gil never fails to use such opportunities to speak a word about his faith in the Lord Jesus Christ. Many of his track trips turn into preaching trips before he gets home. He told reporters in Chicago on the night of breaking the world's record that he was more excited about preaching the next day in Goshen, Ind. than he was in winning the race that night.

If you could have slipped into some of the meetings in which he has spoken from coast to coast in the last few years you would have heard statements such as these:

* * *

"If you live what you preach all can be reached with the Gospel if it is presented through the Spirit's guidance."

* * *

"The best way to run the race of life is to take God as your guide. It's much easier to be an athlete and a Christian than to be an athlete and not a Christian. Defeats make me realize more than ever my dependence on Christ."

* * *

"Track is, has been and always will be secondary with me. My Gospel work comes first."

* * *

"Christianity makes it easier for me to take a beating."

* * *

"By the grace of God, we've been able to do a little running."

* * *

"Folks who doubt the Bible and tear it apart take the heart out of the Bible; they tear up the Master's training rules before they even start life's race, and they can't possibly win."

* * *

"Some people tell me I'm crazy for signing a Bible verse after my name and for witnessing for our Lord whenever I get the chance, but after what He did for us on Calvary we can never do too much for Him."

* * *

"Some Christians are like athletes we often see. They have the ability and power to succeed, but they don't use it in the right way or they don't train right. That's the way it is with some of us Christians. We've got the greatest thing in the world to present but we don't do anything about it."

* * *

"I wanted a baby boy . . . and God was even good to me there. I got one, little Jackie."

* * *

"When a young fellow writes to me to find out how to run the mile I tell him that the first thing he should do is accept the Lord Jesus Christ as his personal Saviour. Then if it's in the Lord's will that he can be a runner, nothing can keep him down. The Lord has a plan and a place for each of us, and it's for us to find Him and to let Him show us His plan for us... After the first step is taken and the way seems open to run, the second step is to determine your weakness and start drilling on that. If you're weak on the dashes spend three or four weeks doing dashes of from 50 to 100 yards during the off season. Three or four weeks before the meet let the speed alone and do basic work, with distance work, to regain the stamina lost in speed work. Each man is an individual and should be trained as such. For the basic work run the 220 yards, 300, 440 and an occasional 660, half-mile or three-fourths mile."

* * *

"Whatever I do in action, word or deed I do to the honor and glory of God, endeavoring to give forth the best I have for Him, the author and finisher of my life."

* * *

Many times, immediately after a race, Gil has been asked by a radio announcer to say a few words over a national hookup. Invariably a word of praise to God for strength in running the race and an appeal comes from his lips. He told a reporter once, "I'm generally a bit winded after a race but the Spirit supplies the words in time of need."

* * *

These past pages and chapters have tried to give you a picture of Gil Dodds, one of the greatest athletes of this century and all time, thanks to the help of God. It's hard to put into words the warmth that flows from the personality of God-guided, God-honoring Gilbert Lothair Dodds, "Miler for Christ." Great as he is in the sports realm, and his greatness there is undisputed, his greatest aim is to be great in the sight of God, usable to win souls to Him through the Lord Jesus Christ.

His clear, unflinching testimony rings out when he asks himself, and you, "Do people want what I've got?" He means it when he says, "It takes a man to be a Christian, and nothing is impossible with God, even the much talked of four-minute mile. Phil. 4:13."

And now, the testimony of God's brightest light in the sports field, Gil Dodds.

Chapter IX

"I RUN FOR CHRIST!"
By Gil Dodds

IT IS a privilege and a pleasure once more to give my testimony for Jesus Christ. Before going another step I wish to say that it has been only through the help of God and His Son, Jesus Christ, that I have been able to do what I have done in track. In every bit of my running there has been but one dominant thought — that in every possible way I might testify for my Lord wherever my racing might take me.

My one dream as a boy was that some day I should be able to run in big-time competition. I used to read of the attainments of Paavo Nurmi, Lloyd Hahn, Glenn Cunningham and many others. The obstacles they met and overcame encouraged me. I often dreamed dreams of some day sinking my spikes into the pine boards of Madison Square Garden, lining up at the starting line with some of the greatest at the starter's command, to hear the gun and lunge forward for the lead and finally feel the tape snap across my chest, the WINNER!

It all seemed in the realm of the unattainable in those early days, as far as I was concerned. It was a far-off vision, a deep burning desire and inward ambition; some even politely called it a "Day Dreamer's Fantasy." But it was at this time in my life, when I was but 13 years old and with my head swimming with the ideas of what I would like to do in life, that a Christian lady — a wonderful Christian lady — crossed my path of life. But what help could this be to the realization of what I had dreamed?

I wanted to be an athlete! She wanted me to be a Christian!

She told me that I had to give my heart to Jesus, that the Christian home in which I lived wasn't going to save me and that my church membership and baptism was far from sufficient. I needed Christ — "The Rose of Sharon, the Bright and Morning Star, the Altogether Lovely One." She also told me I had to realize that I was a sinner, that the wages of sin is death, but that Jesus because of His love for me died upon the cross for ME that I might have EVERLASTING LIFE!!

It was then that I made the initial step which everyone in life must take before having his highest vision in life come true. I yielded my life to Him. He has proven Himself to be the one who is able to do exceeding abundantly above all that I could ask or think for life. My dreams have been realized and I know that it was made possible only through the Lord. He knew my secret desires and He fulfilled them for me. Why I do not know, but I thank Him always that He was so good to me.

To me one of the most glaring misconceptions of the average man on the street is that you can't be a businessman, a professional man, or, most remarkable of all, an athlete, and yet be a Christian.

It's just the other way around! It's the easiest thing in the world to be an athlete and a Christian at the same time. People often have wondered how the two mix and have asked me that question time and time again in my traveling all over the United States. The one rule which I keep before me at all times and which applies to both is found in the Bible in Hebrews 12:1-2,

"Wherefore seeing we also are compassed about with so great a cloud of witnesses, let us lay aside every weight, and the sin that doth so easily beset us, and let us run with patience the race that is set before us,

"Looking unto Jesus the author and finisher of our faith; who for the joy that was set before Him endured the cross, despising the shame, and is set down on the right hand of the throne of God."

In running I put aside all weights. I exercise and control my eating to take off excess poundage first of all. Then I look to my clothing. I have the lightest shoes in my possession to use only in the race. Then I see that my trunks and shirt are just right — not tight and likely to bind me in any way.

So it is in life. We lay aside the sins that are in our lives and hearts and don the full armor of our Lord.

We have to run the race with patience. This is harder than some may think. In a two-mile race we shouldn't go out into the lead and run as fast as we can, or run it as though it were only a one-mile race. And so it is in our spiritual lives. After some have accepted Christ as their Saviour they want to grow to be mature Christians so fast that they don't stop to learn the small truths that could be a help. We get impatient and we take on spiritual tasks which we cannot accomplish. Wait on the Lord; He will teach you these needful things. If not, you may have to learn through bitter defeat, even as I did in many a race.

The last part of the rule is the most important. There is always a finish to a race, the place where victory or defeat is made known. You have to keep your mind and your eyes set on the finish. Some runners look back while they are running and I can't figure out why they do. They lose precious seconds and there is the added danger of losing their footing and perhaps falling.

This applies to life as well. We must keep our eyes on Jesus, "the author and finisher of our faith." He ran His race also, and He had a more difficult race than you or I will ever have. He won, too! That is what makes it glorious for us all. He received the prize. The prizes that I receive in races are corruptible prizes; they are beautiful, have a definite sentimental value and we take pleasure in them.

But the prize that gives to me the greatest pleasure and joy is the prize that Christ won and gave to me and to you who believe on His Name. ETERNAL LIFE! It will never tarnish, be broken, stolen or lost. It is the gift of God through our Lord Jesus Christ.

My orders are to go to athletes. If I should fall down on this I feel that God would hold me accountable.

I find in the Bible many outstanding athletes. David, a man after God's own heart, could shoot the arrow, whirl the sling and track animals as none other. Samson, the strong man of the Bible, feared neither man nor beast but met all in wrestling duels and won. Elijah, the great prophet of old who lived and walked with God, at one time outran a chariot for 26 miles. (I'm going to ask him how he did it when we get to heaven.)

But above all they lived for God.

You perhaps have noticed how many times Paul the Apostle makes reference to athletics in the New Testament — such as "running the race set before us," "pressing toward the mark," "so run that ye may obtain," "fight the good fight of faith," and "we wrestle not against flesh and blood."

So, it seems to me, they who live according to God's rules achieve greatness that endures.

As you may know, my races have not always been victories. I have suffered many defeats. For these I thank the Lord also. His plan has been worked out in my life regardless of my desire. Just as Job and other Old Testament figures suffered setbacks and defeats, so did I, for the Lord had a much greater glory prepared for Himself. A defeat can help you more than a victory at times, and I feel that many of you from your own experience realize that this is true.

He taught me, through these bitter defeats and disappointments, to trust and lean on Him completely. And He has not failed me! Many people whom I had considered as friends have left me at these times of defeat and often it seemed more than I could bear. But the Spirit of God would lead me to read Paul's letter to Timothy. His friends forsook him, too, but he testifies and says, "The Lord stood with me and strengthened me." Our Lord is true to us today as he was always true to His disciples in those early days.

My wife and I pray about everything. Before the Gunder Hagg trip came up we had prayed about it for several weeks, even before it was suggested that we make the tour. We wanted to do His will and felt that whatever came about the Lord would use it to His honor and glory. We had nothing to do with making it possible; we had just one thought in mind — to testify for our Lord at every opportunity on the tour. When the opportunity came we were willing. We had opportunity to testify in Chicago, Los Angeles, San Francisco and other places along with the small personal opportunities which came to us on the train, in restaurants, etc.

As an "ambassador" one must train accordingly. No one can serve God and the world at the same time. Separation is demanded. An ambassador is interested, above all else, in being properly recognized, and to an athlete that means, "Is my name in the world's record book of sports?" I have achieved that satisfaction, but far above all this I praise the Lord that my name is written in the record book of life, through the shed blood of Christ.

Just a word or two to the fellows and boys who are so vitally interested in athletics. From my own personal experience I tell you this — *you can be an athlete and a Christian at the same time.* The outstanding athletes whom it has been my privilege to run against were not only clean fellows but they abided by their Christian beliefs as well. It's this type of athlete that I fear the most to meet — the one who knows Christ and obeys His teaching. They have what I have and we are equal in that respect. It is the athlete who is not a Christian, who smokes and drinks and disobeys all of the rules of training, who gives me the least worry.

Fellows, every outstanding athlete, such as Greg Rice and Gunder Hagg, knows that there are simple yet vital rules that every athlete should and must follow if he hopes to reach the top. These are unwritten rules, but by disobeying them he signs his own death warrant to success.

I won't say here that if you become a Christian that God will make a world champion miler out of you. But I do say this, that if you accept the Lord Jesus Christ as your personal Saviour and yield your life to Him, He will put you just where He wants you to be and you'll be mighty satisfied with it. As I said before, I don't see why God allowed me to satisfy all of my personal desires except that every bit of it has gone to His honor and glory. Let Jesus come into your heart and He'll make you a success in whatever you do; shut Him out and you'll never be the real success you could and should be.

Many people feel that athletics or other worldly pursuits are all that matter in life. They throw aside everything else, even their Christian beliefs. Remember this, always — whenever you stand up for your beliefs, in the Christian spirit, the world will admire you. What can the world give you that God can't give you, plus much more? Sacrifice none of your principles for the world; some may scoff, but they secretly respect you.

Sunday is a different day from the other six. It is a day of rest. Keep it that way! You'll never lose an inch by refusing to compete in events on Sunday.

The Bible gives us some of the greatest promises in the world. Philippians 4:13 strikes me as one of the greatest:

"I can do all things through Christ, which strengtheneth me."

Not of myself, but in Christ! I firmly believe that nothing is impossible with God — not even the much debated four-minute mile. To me the only way it will ever be accomplished is not by man himself but by the will of God and through Christ, who will give the successful runner for that one time strength in exceeding abundance. And then only will it be accomplished for His glory.

What greater friend can one have running beside him in his life's race than Christ? We have so many poor specimens of mankind because it is quite simple for anyone to be a sinner. It takes a man to be a Christian. SO BE A MAN!

Where the Lord wants me after I finish seminary training is up to Him. I'll go anywhere for Him, even to the farthest and most remote island of the world, to the most inhuman tribe of unreached people that is left on this earth, to China, to Africa, or right in my own backyard. Anywhere He puts me in His service is all right with me. All that I am or have accomplished and all that I ever hope to be I owe to God and to Him do I give all of the glory and credit. I praise God, from whom cometh all my strength, knowing that "Christ is the same yesterday, today and forever," and that "He is a friend that sticketh closer than a brother."

Is your name in the Record book of Life?